Lectio Divina BIBLE STUDY

THE MASS
in Scripture

Lectio Divina BIBLE STUDY

THE MASS
in Scripture

STEPHEN J. BINZ

Our Sunday Visitor Publishing Division
Our Sunday Visitor, Inc.
Huntington, IN 46750

Copyright © 2011 by Stephen J. Binz.
Published 2011.

16 15 14 13 12 11   2 3 4 5 6 7 8 9

Our Sunday Visitor Publishing Division
Our Sunday Visitor, Inc.
200 Noll Plaza
Huntington, IN 46750

bookpermissions@osv.com
1-800-348-2440

ISBN 978-1-59276-829-5 (Inventory No. T1132)
LCCN: 2010942586

Interior and cover design by Amanda Falk
Cover image by Shutterstock

PRINTED IN THE UNITED STATES OF AMERICA

ENDORSEMENTS FOR *LECTIO DIVINA BIBLE STUDY: THE MASS IN SCRIPTURE*, BY STEPHEN J. BINZ

Stephen Binz' *The Mass in Scripture* provides every reader with an opportunity to learn how to pray the parts of the Mass with devotion and understanding. Binz' straightforward writing allows readers of all levels to learn what the Council set out as one of the great goals of its liturgical reform: the increased participation of the faithful at every Mass.

> — **Most Reverend Timothy M. Dolan, Archbishop of New York**

The Mass in Scripture is an insightful resource for individual and group study by Catholics who wish to further their understanding of the biblical roots of the Mass and the meaning of the coming changes in the Mass prayers. Stephen Binz has provided a well-organized and clearly written guide that can only heighten appreciation for the inexhaustible riches of our Catholic Mass.

> — **His Eminence Donald Cardinal Wuerl, Archbishop of Washington**

In his book, *The Mass in Scripture*, Stephen J. Binz does a brilliant job in using Lectio Divina to help Catholics grow in a deeper understanding of and appreciation for the Mass. His writing is strongly based in Scripture and draws readers into a deeper celebration of the Mass and a commitment to live out their lives as a eucharistic people.

> — **Most Rev. Gregory M. Aymond, Archbishop of New Orleans, Chair of the USCCB Committee on Divine Worship**

Stephen Binz invites us to move beyond the surface words we say to the meaning of what we do. He has provided a remarkable tool for just such reflection. Using an ancient pattern of reflection, prayer, and action, and grounding his work in the historical and theological underpinnings of what we celebrate today, he provides a unique exploration of the various parts of the eucharistic liturgy, at once solid and accessible. Individuals and groups alike will profit immensely from this book.

> — **Kathleen Hughes, R.S.C.J., former Professor of Word and Worship at the Catholic Theological Union, Mission Consultant in the Network of Sacred Heart Schools**

Every Catholic would like to get more out of the Mass, and the revised translation is encouraging everyone to think more deeply about the words we hear and say. Stephen Binz provides a very helpful guide for those who wish to enter this process prayerfully, in community, and with the Bible in hand. This book will give the reader an experience of Christ and the church that will enrich every celebration of the Mass.

> — **Rev. Paul Turner, Pastor of St. Munchin Church, Diocese of Kansas City-St. Joseph, Facilitator for the International Commission on English in the Liturgy**

A very serious yet "user friendly" prayerful appreciation of the Eucharist based on the Scriptures. Readers who apply themselves to the guided prayer and group discussions outlined here will have their experience of the celebration of the Eucharist enriched beyond words. Particularly helpful is the author's familiarity with the Old Testament bases for Christian worship. This initial offering in the "Lifelong Mystagogy in the Catholic Way" series augurs well for what promises to be a series that has the potential to change minds, hearts, and souls.

— Rev. Msgr. Kevin Irwin, Dean of the School of Theology and Religious studies,
The Catholic University of America

The Mass in Scripture yokes solid biblical scholarship, liturgical history, and theology, and pastoral insight into a wonderful resource for individuals and groups wishing to deepen their appreciation for the celebration of the Eucharist in the Roman Rite. Adapting the monastic meditative savoring of Scripture to the texts and ceremonies of the Mass, Stephen Binz both instructs and models how eucharistic mystagogy might be fruitfully engaged. It is one of those rare books that could be used with profit by clergy and religious professionals, cradle Catholics, and new initiates.

— Rev. Jan Michael Joncas, liturgical theologian and composer,
Associate Professor of Catholic Studies, University of St. Thomas

This book, the first in the *Lectio Divina Bible Study* series, is a timely gift to the People of God who worship in English. The Lectio Divina framework, as Stephen Binz applies it, is a marvelously apt guide for preparing individuals and worshiping communities for the new translation of the Roman Missal and for a more profound participation in the liturgy. The biblical and liturgical scholarship is solid yet accessible. Binz' approach is creative, non-polemical, and traditional in the best sense of the word.

— Judith M. Kubicki, C.S.S.F., liturgical theologian,
Associate Professor of Theology, Fordham University

Stephen Binz' timely book provides an integrated approach into the experience of worship, employing the Scriptures as a pathway to unfold the mysteries which engage the worshiper. Utilizing a creative method based on lectio divina to uncover the biblical roots of worship, Binz invites the reader to reflect on both the Tradition of the Church and personal memory, illuminating the experience of each part of the Mass. As a result, readers are led to discover the implications worship has for their lives in the world.

— Rev. Thomas Ranzino, Pastor of St. Jean Vianney Church,
Director of the Office of Worship, Diocese of Baton Rouge

Contents

Welcome to Lectio Divina Bible Study   9

Section I — Overview of *The Mass in Scripture*   17

Section II — Honoring God in Covenant Worship   29
     Lesson 1.   The Defining Drama and Memorial Feast of Passover   31
     Lesson 2.   The Book of the Covenant and the Blood of Sacrifice   35
     Lesson 3.   Sacrifice Offered for the Atonement of Sin   40
     Lesson 4.   A Thanksgiving Offering for Deliverance   45
     Lesson 5.   Encountering the Risen Christ in Word and Sacrament   50
     Lesson 6.   Worshiping the Lamb in Heaven's Liturgy   55
     Group Session Guide for Section II   59

Section III — Introductory Rites of the Mass   61
     Lesson 7.   Processing to the House and Altar of God   63
     Lesson 8.   Marked with the Sign of the Cross
                 in the Name of the Trinity   68
     Lesson 9.   The Grace of our Lord Jesus Christ Be with Your Spirit   73
     Lesson 10. Lord, Have Mercy, for I Have Sinned   78
     Lesson 11. Singing "Glory to God in the Highest"
                 and "Peace on Earth"   83
     Lesson 12. Praying to the Father, through Jesus Christ,
                 in the Holy Spirit   87
     Group Session Guide for Section III   91

Section IV — The Liturgy of the Word   93
     Lesson 13. The Word of the Lord Spoken to Moses   95
     Lesson 14. Ezra Proclaims the Torah to God's Listening People   100
     Lesson 15. The Liturgy of the Word in the Synagogue of Nazareth   105

Lesson 16. Philip Guides the Ethiopian to Understand the Scripture   109
Lesson 17. Professing the Faith of the Church   113
Lesson 18. Voicing the Prayers of God's Faithful People   118
Group Session Guide for Section IV   122

Section V — The Liturgy of the Eucharist   **125**
Lesson 19. Presenting the Gifts of Bread and Wine   127
Lesson 20. Holy, Holy, Holy is the Lord of Hosts   132
Lesson 21. Jesus' Prayer of Consecration to the Father   137
Lesson 22. The Institution of Eucharistic Worship   142
Lesson 23. A Pure Offering to God among All the Nations   147
Lesson 24. Christ's One Sacrifice Offered for All   152
Group Session Guide for Section V   157

Section VI — The Communion Rite and Dismissal   **159**
Lesson 25. Awaiting the Blessed Hope, We Pray as Jesus Taught Us   161
Lesson 26. Offering the Sign of Peace to One Another   166
Lesson 27. Lamb of God Who Takes Away the Sin of the World   171
Lesson 28. Eating His Body and Drinking His Blood   176
Lesson 29. The Many Become the One Body of Christ   180
Lesson 30. Blessing and Commissioning God's People   185
Group Session Guide for Section VI   190

Welcome to Lectio Divina Bible Study

LIFELONG MYSTAGOGY IN THE CATHOLIC WAY ▨

Lectio Divina Bible Study is designed to assist Catholic Christians in the lifelong process of understanding the faith and living it more intentionally. Through an immersion in sacred Scripture, disciples will grow and mature in their calling, continually deepening their appreciation and practice of the Christian mysteries. Ongoing volumes will focus on worship, prayer, spiritual practices, and active commitment, helping participants make the Catholic Christian way of life more fully their own.

Mystagogy is a Greek word meaning "education in the mysteries." Initiation into the Easter mysteries should lead Christians into a lifelong process of ongoing conversion and growth in understanding. Though the early church adopted this term to refer to the formal process of leading new Christians into a deeper grasp of the sacraments they experienced at Easter, the process of mystagogy does not end after the fifty days of the Easter season. This education in the paschal mystery of Christ continues throughout life's pilgrimage and is the task of every member of the church.

Lectio Divina Bible Study utilizes inspired Scripture, along with the tradition and scholarship of the church, to lead maturing Catholic Christians into an ever deeper relationship with Jesus Christ and an appreciation of the gospel's challenges. These books are guides for life's journey, helping users to place the paschal mystery at the heart of life and live more fully in Christ.

Each work in this series employs the tradition of lectio divina, the church's most ancient way of reading Scripture. The lessons lead the reader through five movements: listening, understanding, reflecting, praying, and acting. Contained within each of these lessons are Scripture texts, commentary on the texts, suggestions for personal reflection, ideas for prayer, and suggestions for actualizing the text in the context of daily life.

These books are designed for use by individuals studying on their own or within groups. They are self-contained, with all the information necessary to be used for an individual or group process. All follow the same methodology, beginning with a general overview of the topic and a short practice of the study's method, and followed by five main sections, each of which contain six biblical lessons.

THE ANCIENT ART OF LECTIO DIVINA ▨

This time-tested way of reading Scripture was nurtured through the centuries of Christianity, and is today experiencing a worldwide revival among all the people of God. Through the movements of lectio divina, we are led to an encounter with God, who speaks to us through the pages of the inspired text, inviting from us a personal response and a gradual transformation of life.

The heart of this practice is an understanding of the Bible's inspiration, the belief that God is the Author, or source, of Scripture. Though written by human writers in various periods of history, God's Spirit moved within the writers so that the biblical words speak God's word to his people. But inspiration does not just refer to the work of God's Spirit at the time the texts were written. It is an ongoing reality within the sacred pages. The Scriptures remain inspired, and when read in faith today, they are filled with the Spirit of God.

The ancient art of lectio divina is not a rigid system or a set of required steps for reading the Bible. It is, rather, a way of approaching the sacred text with faith, openheartedness, reverence, and expectation. The reader trusts that God is present and speaks to his people through the inspired word, working profoundly within our minds and hearts.

Throughout history this practice of sacred reading has taken many forms through the writings of the saints and spiritual masters. Words such as *lectio, cogitatio, meditatio, compassio, oratio, contemplatio, consolatio, discretio, deliberatio,* and *operatio* have filled books of spiritual literature to express aspects of this ancient practice. Lectio Divina Bible Study utilizes five terms to describe these movements and lead readers into a transforming experience: listening, understanding, reflecting, praying, and acting.

LISTENING

Reading a sacred text in this tradition means reading with expectancy, trusting that God will speak his word to us through the page. St. Benedict, in his monastic *Rule*, described this kind of reading as hearing "with the ear of our heart." God speaks and we listen.

The key to this deep listening is reading the biblical text with as little prejudgment as possible, as if we were hearing it for the first time. We can't listen fully to God if we think we already know what the text is going to tell us. Rather, this expectant reading requires that we create a space within ourselves for the new insight and wisdom God wants to give us through the sacred page.

This deep listening requires careful, fully attentive reading, engaging our mind, our imagination, our emotions, and our will. It can be helpful to read aloud, so that we see the words with our eyes, form them with our lips, and hear them with our ears. We savor the words of the sacred literature, appreciating the images, envisioning the scene, feeling the sentiments, allowing the words to move from our heads to our hearts.

UNDERSTANDING

Seeking to comprehend the meaning of a text is an important part of encountering God and being changed by that encounter. The church's early theologians show us that there is no clear distinction between studying Scripture and reading it prayerfully. The more we come to understand the text with our minds, the more we are capable of being changed by the text.

We will be able to probe the fullest meaning of the text the more we comprehend something of its original context — historical, cultural, literary, and religious. When, where, and why was the author writing? Most importantly, how did the writer's faith manifest itself in the text and what kind of faith response does the writer expect from the reader? Seeking to understand the faith dimension of the text helps us transcend the original circumstances in which it was written, and allows us to see the lasting significance and validity it has for all of us.

Bible studies and biblical commentaries can be a great help to understanding. Listening to the text with the understanding of the church and with some basic insights of biblical scholarship can assure us that our comprehension is true and faithful. This listening to the text for understanding, with its multiple layers of meaning and rich history of interpretation, forms the foundation on which we can begin to experience its transforming potential.

REFLECTING

Even though the Bible was written ages ago, its pages always have meanings and messages for us today. Our challenge is to find connections between the text of yesterday and the today of our lives. By reflecting on the sacred texts, we link the biblical truth of scriptural passages to the experience of faith in the world in which we live.

Because the biblical literature is the word of God, it has a richness of meaning that can be discovered by individuals in every age and in every culture. Its personal message can be received by every reader who listens to the word in the context of his or her daily experiences. We should read the text until it becomes like a mirror, reflecting some of our own thoughts, questions, challenges, and experiences.

Mary of Nazareth is the best model for this type of reflecting on God's word: "Mary treasured all these words and pondered them in her heart" (Luke 2:19). To "ponder" suggests that the word has enough gravity to shape and expand the understanding of the heart. The word of God can form our hearts when we allow it to rest within us and gradually mold our desires, insights, and judgments.

PRAYING

After listening carefully and reflectively to God's word in Scripture, we naturally reach a point in which we want to respond. Prayer is our heartfelt response to God's word. In this way, lectio divina becomes fundamentally a dialogue with God: we listen to God, then we respond to God in prayer.

Our prayerful response to God flows directly from our biblical reading, understanding, and reflecting. In this way our prayer is enriched through the vocabulary, images, and sentiments of the biblical text as it is joined with the thoughts, needs, and desires arising within us. As a grace-filled and Spirit-led response to God, our prayer becomes increasingly personal and intimate.

After responding to God with word-filled prayer, words gradually become less helpful and unnecessary. We are then often led by God into a wordless silence, an effortless resting in God's presence. This type of prayer is traditionally called contemplation. We simply end our prayer by receiving and accepting the transforming embrace of the One who has led us to the quiet moment.

ACTING

Every biblical passage offers a call, or challenge, to those who listen to its sacred words. After prayerfully listening to God through a passage of Scripture, we should be impacted in a way that makes a difference in the way we live. In addition to drawing us inward to reflection and prayer, the word of God impels us outward to those people and situations in need of God's light and compassionate presence. By acting on Scripture we become, as James says, "doers of the word, and not merely hearers" (James 1:22).

These active changes in our lives are the fruit of lectio divina. Occasionally the changes are remarkable; more often they are subtle. We gradually become aware that the fruit of studying the Bible is the fruit of the Spirit: "love, joy, peace, patience, kindness, generosity, faithfulness, gentleness, and self-control" (Galatians 5:22–23). When we begin to notice this fruit in the way we live each day, we will know that the word of God is working within us. We become more effective members of the body of Christ in the world and witnesses to God's kingdom.

Personal Use of Lectio Divina Bible Study

- Make Bible study a regular part of your life. Study one lesson each day, or as often as you can according to the circumstances of your life.

- Find a regular time during the day that can become a pattern for you. Choose a quiet and comfortable place where you will be undisturbed.

- Make your time for study a sacred time. Set it apart by calling on the guidance of the Holy Spirit.

- Study slowly and carefully. Don't hesitate to mark up this book with notes, highlights, underlining, circles, or whatever will help you pay attention and remember the text and commentary.

- Follow the movements of lectio divina outlined in each lesson. Realize that this is only a tentative guide for the more important movements of God's Spirit within you.

- Write out your responses as suggested in the lesson. The act of writing will help you clarify your thoughts, deepen your understanding, and bring new insights.

- Approach your study with expectancy, trusting that God will indeed work deeply within you through his word.

- Try to be accountable to at least one other person for your regular practice of lectio divina. Tell a friend, spouse, spiritual director, or pastor about your experience in order to receive encouragement and affirmation.

Lectio Divina Bible Study for Groups

Churches and other faith communities may choose to adopt Lectio Divina Bible Study and support its use in a variety of ways. Since this study is ideally suited both for personal use by individuals and for group use, communities are able to respect the many ways people desire to make this Bible study a personal priority. By encouraging an array of options for participation, communities will be able to encourage this form of ongoing faith formation by many people in the community.

OFFERING A VARIETY OF OPTIONS TO ENCOURAGE PARTICIPATION ■

- Facilitate the formation of small groups that meet regularly at church facilities or in homes. These groups may meet at different times throughout the week to offer convenient options for people in different circumstances.

- Provide groups for people with similar connections: young adults, retired seniors, parents with young children, etc. These groupings may encourage a deeper level of personal reflection among members.

- Offer this study to people who want to participate alone. Respect the fact that many don't have the time or desire to join a group. Include these people in the invitation and prayerful encouragement of the whole community.

- Consider other creative ways of establishing communities for study. Support the establishment of online communities or Internet social networks for this study. Participants might want to commit themselves to sending a text message or e-mail to the group offering their insights after reflecting on each lesson.

- Personally invite people to participate, encourage them through pastoral leadership, offer a public sign-up after the Sunday liturgy, and make the study a priority within the faith community.

FORMING SMALL GROUPS FOR WEEKLY SESSIONS ■

The personal use of Lectio Divina Bible Study may be integrated into a process of faith formation for small groups. Through the thoughts, reflections, prayers, and experiences of the other members of the group, each individual comes to understand the lessons more profoundly. By sharing wisdom and experience in a faith-filled group of people, individuals enrich the lives of one another.

Small groups are best formed when people are encouraged and supported by a church's pastoral leadership and personally welcomed into these small communities.

Personally directed invitations are most effective for convincing people to add another activity to their busy lives. Groups composed of no more than a dozen people are best for this experience. It is preferable to give people with various needs a variety of days and times from which to choose.

The group process should never take the place of one's own individual study and reflection. Rather, a weekly communal practice is an ideal extension and continuation of personal, daily listening, understanding, reflecting, praying, and acting. As a member of a group, each person takes responsibility for studying the material for six days on their own and meeting with the group once a week for six weeks.

GROUP DISCUSSION IN SIX SESSIONS

- Begin each group session with hospitality and welcome. Name tags are helpful if group members don't know one another. Offer any announcements or instructions before entering the spirit of focused discussion and listening to others.

- The first group session is based on the material of section I, the overview. Group members read each section and discuss the questions that follow. The last section of the overview offers group members an experience of the five movements: listening, understanding, reflecting, praying, and acting. Simply follow each step as a group.

- The group sessions for the following weeks are based on the material of sections II through VI that individuals will have completed during the week.

- After sections II through VI, you will find a "Group Session Guide" for discussing the six lessons prepared individually during the week. Don't linger too long on any single question, so that the full range of questions are covered from all six lessons.

- An alternate way of spending the group time is to ask the following question for each of the six lessons: "What is most significant for you from this lesson?" Members may discuss an insight from the Scripture or commentary, their response from one of the reflections, or the prayer or action that was particularly helpful or provocative.

- Conclude the session with a form of prayer that is agreed upon by the group. Suggest that members first offer prayers of thanksgiving aloud to God for the insights and particular ways they were moved by the lessons of the week. This may be followed by prayers of petition in which members may pray for their own needs and those of others, as well as for the grace to act upon any decisions or resolutions that the lessons have moved them to make.

- Before departing each week, encourage group members to complete each of the next six lessons during the week ahead.

- At the end of the final session, members may want to celebrate their completion in some way and then decide to work together on another Lectio Divina Bible Study or another type of study for faith formation.

SUGGESTIONS FOR PARTICIPATING IN THE GROUP

- It is important to have someone guide the process of the group. This facilitator directs the discussion, helping the group keep the discussion on time and on track. The facilitator need not be an expert, but simply a person with the human skills necessary to guide a group. This role may be rotated among members of the group, if desired.

- Always try to complete your individual study of each lesson before the group meeting. This will give you more to contribute to the group. But don't worry if you have not completed each lesson. Come anyway and learn from others.

- The spirit of the group session should be that of a conversation, with members sharing their learning and offering a supportive ear to one another.

- When participating in the group, you should freely offer thoughts, insights, and feelings about your learning. Avoid distractions by focusing on the movements of each lesson.

- Offer everyone in the group an opportunity to share their insights. When discussing personal thoughts, try not to use "I" language and be cautious about giving advice to others.

- Listen attentively to the other members of the group to learn from their insights. Encourage others by following up on comments with supportive statements.

- Avoid dispute, debate, and doctrinaire hairsplitting. Opposition, division, and self-assertion destroy the supportive bond of the group.

- When disagreements arise, it is often wise to "agree to disagree." An inflexible, pedantic attitude blocks the way to a vital and fulfilling understanding of the lesson.

Section I

Overview of *The Mass in Scripture*

From the procession to the altar and the Sign of the Cross to the final blessing and sending forth, the eucharistic liturgy of the church is a mosaic of words, images, and actions drawn from sacred Scripture. In the Mass, we address God in words that have been given to us through his Holy Spirit, and God then comes to us — teaching, saving, and sanctifying us — again through the inspired words of Scripture.

The Bible leads us to the altar of the Lord. The Mass is the Bible in action, the saving truths and events of Scripture made present and real before us in the eucharistic liturgy. The purpose and meaning of the sacred texts are fulfilled in this solemn mystery of the church's faith. The new and eternal life that Scripture proclaims is truly experienced in the holy sacrament of the altar.

Celebrated in every epoch for two millennia and expressed in every culture from east to west, north to south, the Eucharist offers humanity's best to God. Eucharistic worship has inspired the finest works of human creativity, from the house churches of the early Christians to the magnificent basilicas and splendid cathedrals of later centuries. Enhanced by architecture of diverse cultural styles, a rich tradition of painting, iconography, sculpture, and a diverse heritage of sacred music, the church's liturgy has motivated artistic vision to honor the divine made flesh in sacramental mystery.

Though the Mass may seem complicated to outside observers, its structural design is really quite simple and is derived from the rites of ancient Israel. It is composed of two essential and interrelated parts: The proclamation of Scripture and the ritual at the altar. In both movements we encounter the risen Christ and are formed into his church.

The multi-dimensional depth of this ancient ritual is expressed through the different names it possesses. "The Lord's Supper" (1 Cor 11:20; Rev 19:9) recalls the founding meal that Jesus ate with his disciples on the eve of his sacrificial death and anticipates the wedding banquet of the Lamb in the future Jerusalem. "The breaking of the bread" (Acts 2:42) is the name given by the early Christians of Jerusalem for their communal worship in which they recognized the Risen Lord (Luke 24:35). "Holy Communion" expresses the unity we experience in Christ as the broken bread and cup of blessing become a communion in his body and blood (1 Cor 10:16–17). "The Divine Liturgy" in the church of the East evokes the fact that the public worship of God's people finds its most intense expression in the eucharistic ritual, while "the Mass" in the church of the West brings to mind the sending forth (*missio*) that concludes the eucharistic liturgy, as participants are commissioned to serve Christ in the world. "Eucharist" comes from the Greek verb *eucharistein*, "to give thanks" (1 Cor 11:24), recalling the Jewish blessings that give thanks for God's work of creation, redemption, and sanctification. Each name evokes diverse aspects of the infinite riches of the eucharistic liturgy.

There is no better lifelong mystagogy than to reflect on this divine gift in light of Scripture. Through the gradual, reflective process of mystagogy, we will study these sacred texts and use them to deepen our understanding of the Eucharist we experience. Through this biblical study we will grow to better understand the mystery of our faith and mature in our Christian calling.

- In what sense can we say that the Bible and the Mass were made for each other?

- What is most puzzling to me about the church's liturgy? What would I like to understand more?

 # Eucharistic Liturgy in the Early Church ▉

The liturgy of the church, of which we receive glimpses throughout the New Testament, is described by the second-century theologian Justin Martyr. In his *First Apology*, written in about AD 155 to the emperor Antonius Pius, he explains Christian beliefs and practices. He describes what eucharistic worship looked like in his church in Rome. Justin writes that the Christians gather on the day called Sunday because "Jesus Christ our Savior on the same day rose from the dead." On that day "all who live in cities or in the country gather together in one place."

In the first part of the service, "the memoirs of the apostles or the writings of the prophets are read, as long as time permits." This consists of the reading of Scripture, both the Scriptures of Israel, which we know as the Old Testament, and the new writings of the apostles, which we know as the gospels, letters, and other New Testament writings. The presider then offers a homily based on these readings: "the president verbally instructs and exhorts to the imitation of these good things." After this, the assembly rises together and offers prayers of intercession, "hearty prayers in common for ourselves ... and for all others in every place." The prayers are then followed by the exchange of a kiss (the Kiss of Peace).

In the second part of the service, bread and wine are brought forward, and over them the presider offers the Eucharistic Prayer. Justin describes it thus:

> There is then brought to the president of the brethren bread and a cup of wine mixed with water; and he taking them, gives praise and glory to the Father of the universe, through the name of the Son and of the Holy Spirit, and offers thanks at considerable length for our being accounted worthy to receive these things at his hands. And when he has concluded the prayers and thanksgivings, all the people present express their assent by saying Amen.

Justin describes the communion as a distribution and a participation in the elements over which the presider has prayed: "There is a distribution to each, and a participation of that over which thanks have been given, and to those who are absent a portion is sent by the deacons." He says that this food is shared only by those baptized into Christ, those who share the beliefs of the church and live according to Christ's teaching.

> And this food is called among us *Eucharistia* [the Eucharist], of which no one is allowed to partake but the one who believes that the things which we teach are true, and who has been washed with the washing that is for the remission of sins, and unto regeneration, and who is so living as Christ has enjoined.

Justin goes on to identify the food of the Eucharist as "the flesh and blood" of Jesus. He states that this food, through "transmutation," nourishes the blood and flesh of the participants. This teaching is in faithfulness to the teachings of Jesus passed on by the apostles through the gospels.

> For not as common bread and common drink do we receive these; but in like manner as Jesus Christ our Savior, having been made flesh by the Word of God, had both flesh and blood for our salvation, so likewise have we been taught that the food which is blessed by the prayer of His word, and from which our blood and flesh by transmutation are nourished, is the flesh and blood of that Jesus who was made flesh. For the apostles, in the memoirs composed by them, which are called Gospels, have thus delivered unto us what was enjoined upon them; that Jesus took bread, and when He had given thanks, said, This do in remembrance of Me, this is My body; and that, after the same manner, having taken the cup and given thanks, He said, This is My blood; and gave it to them alone.

Lastly, Justin's writings state that after the liturgy, the Christians continually remind one another of what they have shared and what their Eucharist has enjoined upon them: "And the wealthy among us help the needy; and we always keep together; and for all things wherewith we are supplied, we bless the Maker of all through His Son Jesus Christ, and through the Holy Spirit." They give thanks to God for all things and willingly give to those in need.

> And they who are well to do, and willing, give what each thinks fit; and what is collected is deposited with the president, who succors the orphans and widows and those who, through sickness or any other cause, are in want, and those who are in bonds and the strangers sojourning among us, and in a word takes care of all who are in need.

Notice that the structure of worship seems firmly in place: the Liturgy of the Word and the Liturgy of the Eucharist. The proclamation of Scripture, followed by the homily, intercessory prayers, and the kiss of peace make up the first part of the service. The liturgy at the altar consists of bringing bread and wine to the table, an extended eucharistic prayer including praise and thanksgiving to the Father and the words of institution of Jesus from the gospels, and the participation in the body and blood of Christ for those who have been baptized.

For Justin and the early Christians, the eucharistic liturgy was not simply a ceremony. It defined the church. It was the way in which Christ was present to his people across time. In the Eucharist, the Word made flesh continued to give his flesh and blood for them and to dwell with them, just as he does today.

- Which elements of Justin's description of the eucharistic liturgy most closely parallel the Mass as it is celebrated today?

- Why was the eucharistic food to be shared only by those who have been baptized and who share the faith of the church?

The Church's Summit and Font ▓

Worship of God in the Mass is the most distinctive activity of Christ's church and the central focus of a vital Christian life. It is the summit toward which all the church's activity is directed and also the font from which the church's life flows. In the New Testament, the celebration of the Eucharist by the community is assumed, and it forms the background out of which all of those writings were formed. For this reason, none of the New Testament texts offer a systematic explanation of the method and meaning of the church's worship.

Scripture offers numerous clues and suggestions that lead us to a more comprehensive understanding of Christian worship in its essential form. Our understanding is mistaken if we try to reduce the liturgical practice of the church to a single, all-inclusive meaning. Rather, by studying the Scriptures, we can define several dimensions of meaning within the eucharistic mystery that we call the Mass. Here we briefly describe five of these facets that will be explored more fully throughout this study.

1. **Thanksgiving.** The thanksgiving sacrifice of the Old Testament was offered by a person whose life had been redeemed or delivered from a great danger. The person who had been delivered would express his gratitude to God by celebrating a sacrificial meal with bread and wine among family and friends. During the meal, a psalm was sung that narrated the impending danger and plea for deliverance followed by thanksgiving and praise to God. The annual Passover was the collective thanksgiving sacrifice for Israel. In the narrative accounts of the Last Supper, Jesus first gives thanks over the bread and wine. The word Eucharist, which means "thanksgiving," is the Greek word used in these texts. The Eucharist became the church's central act of thanksgiving to God for the gifts of creation and for the redemptive death and resurrection of Christ.

2. **Remembrance.** As the Passover makes the exodus of Israel and its liberating effects present for every generation, the Eucharist makes the death and resurrection of Jesus and its saving effects present each time it is celebrated. These sacramental actions are not just a form of mental recall. Though both actions happened once in the past, they are made present again or re-presented each time they are commemorated in sacred ritual. Jesus' actions in the Upper Room were accompanied by the instruction to "do this in remembrance of me." Each time the church celebrates the eucharistic liturgy, the saving events it commemorates become contemporary to those engaged in it. Through this covenant renewal, the everlasting sacrifice of Christ is made truly present in every generation.

3. **Covenant sacrifice.** In the Old Testament, sacrifices involved offerings of animals as well as grains, bread, and wine. The sacrifice often included a holy meal, which completed the offering and gave participants a way to share in the benefits of the sacrifice. Covenants were always sealed with the blood of sacrifice, and the periodic renewal of a covenant consisted of the proclamation of Scripture, a sacrificial offering, and a sacred meal. The sacrifice of Jesus was so decisive for humanity's salvation that he offered himself and returned to the Father only after he left us a means of sharing in that sacrifice. At the Last Supper, Jesus instituted the new covenant sealed in his blood. As we renew this covenant in every Mass, Jesus offers his body "given for you" and his blood "poured out for you." His one sacrifice is sacramentally re-presented on the altars of his church throughout the world.

4. **Communion.** Paul describes the eucharistic liturgy of the church as a real participation in the risen life of Christ: "The cup of blessing that we bless, is it not a sharing in the blood of Christ? The bread which we break, is it not a sharing in the body of Christ?" The Greek word for "sharing" is *koinonia*, an intimate communion. The one who gave himself completely for us on the cross continues to give himself, to share his life completely with us. John tells us that the Word made flesh gives us his flesh to eat and his blood to drink for our eternal life. In the Eucharist, Christ is truly present — body and blood, soul and divinity — giving himself for our spiritual food and nourishment.

5. **Anticipation of Christ's return.** The church's liturgy not only looks back to the Last Supper and the Lord's passion, it also looks forward to the banquet in that new world God wants to create. By offering us a foretaste of the fullness of joy promised to us, the Eucharist allows us a glimpse of heaven on earth and plants a confident hope in our daily commitments. It offers us a deep sense of responsibility for creation, obliging us to seek God's will on earth, committing us to transforming the world in harmony with God's plan. The exclamation *Maranatha* ("Come, Lord!") is drawn from the eucharistic liturgy of the apostolic church and appears at the end of the book of Revelation. It expresses the simultaneous belief in Christ's eucharistic presence with the church and hope for his glorious coming.

All of these dimensions of meaning are found simultaneously in the eucharistic liturgy of the church. The Eucharist also unites the vertical and horizontal dimensions of our existence, so that our lives may truly be marked by the cross. The vertical dimension is manifested as Christ offers his eternal sacrifice to the Father and we receive its saving grace, as the church on earth joins in the eternal worship of the angels and saints of heaven. The horizontal dimension is evident as the church shares the sacred banquet of communion in his body and blood, as those who receive the risen Christ become his living body in the world. Because the liturgy is simultaneously both a vertical and horizontal event, the place around which disciples gather is, at the same time, the altar of Christ's sacrifice and the table of the Lord.

The liturgy also elevates the dimension of time. The memory of the past and the expectation of a glorious future come together in the eternal, eucharistic moment. In the Mass, God wants to make us alive in a new way, like he did for Jesus on the first day of the week. As we receive God's creative word and are nourished by Christ's body and blood, we are filled with the Holy Spirit and experience the new creation. We can proclaim to the world that forgiveness has been given and death has been defeated. We don't have to wait until after death to receive eternal life; we already possess it in our sacramental union with Christ.

- In what way to I experience the eucharistic liturgy as the summit and font of the church's life?

- Which dimension of meaning do I want to understand better in my study of the Mass?

Proclaiming the Lord's Death Until He Comes ■

In this first session of lectio divina, we seek a deeper experience of the church's eucharistic liturgy through reflecting on an ancient biblical text. Our first Scripture passage is probably the church's oldest existing teaching on the Eucharist, written in the middle of the first century. With this Scripture, we will allow the ancient art of lectio divina to guide us as we listen, understand, reflect, pray, and act.

Listening

Hear what Paul is teaching the church at Corinth. Listen carefully as if you were gathered at Eucharist on the Lord's Day hearing the newly arrived letter from Paul.

1 Corinthians 11:17–29

[17]Now in the following instructions I do not commend you, because when you come together it is not for the better but for the worse. [18]For, to begin with, when you come together as a church, I hear that there are divisions among you; and to some extent I believe it. [19]Indeed, there have to be factions among you, for only so will it become clear who among you are genuine. [20]When you come together, it is not really to eat the Lord's supper. [21]For when the time comes to eat, each of you goes ahead with your own supper, and one goes hungry and another becomes drunk. [22]What! Do you not have homes to eat and drink in? Or do you show contempt for the church of God and humiliate those who have nothing? What should I say to you? Should I commend you? In this matter I do not commend you!

[23]For I received from the Lord what I also handed on to you, that the Lord Jesus on the night when he was betrayed took a loaf of bread, [24]and when he had given thanks, he broke it and said, "This is my body that is for you. Do this in remembrance of me." [25]In the same way he took the cup also, after supper, saying, "This cup is the new covenant in my blood. Do this, as often as you drink it, in remembrance of me." [26]For as often as you eat this bread and drink the cup, you proclaim the Lord's death until he comes.

[27]Whoever, therefore, eats the bread or drinks the cup of the Lord in an unworthy manner will be answerable for the body and blood of the Lord. [28]Examine yourselves, and only then eat of the bread and drink of the cup. [29]For all who eat and drink without discerning the body, eat and drink judgment against themselves.

UNDERSTANDING

After letting these words of Paul sink in, continue searching for their significance in the life of the early church.

The eucharistic words and gestures of Christ's Last Supper have come to us in four different forms: three in the gospel narratives and one here in Paul's letter (vv. 23-25). Paul states that he "handed on" to the church in Corinth what he received from the Lord. This faithful handing on of what was received from the apostolic foundation of the church is called tradition.

Paul presents himself as a link in this chain of eucharistic tradition that Jesus himself gave to the church. Paul challenges the church to be faithful to what was handed on to them. The community must make the words and actions of Christ its own, faithfully carrying on the tradition as a vital element of its commitment in Christ.

When the Christians of Corinth gathered for "the Lord's Supper," it was set in the context of a meal, just as the Last Supper of Jesus with his disciples. The assemblies consisted of rich and poor, slaves and free persons, women and men, all meeting together in one of the larger homes of the community. But this gathering of the church in Corinth became plagued with problems. Divisions and factions developed (v. 18). Some went hungry while others indulged (v. 21). The poor were humiliated because they had nothing to eat (v. 22). Paul was appalled that social hierarchies and social factions had infiltrated the church's central act of worship. The assembly was not even worthy to be called "the Lord's Supper" (v. 20). The words and gestures given by Christ to his church had become empty because the community was no longer doing what Jesus did, giving his life in self-emptying love. He had given the Eucharist to his church as an expression of generous self-giving, a communion in which people formerly divided by race, class, and gender became one body in Christ.

Paul reminds the community of the words and actions of Jesus at the Last Supper in order to correct its understanding and practice of the Eucharist. Jesus said that the broken bread is "my body that is for you" and that the cup is "the new covenant in my blood" (vv. 24–25). His redemptive death for others and his inauguration of the new covenant is the central meaning of the Eucharist. His saving death on the cross and the pouring out of his blood is the sacrifice made present at the community's Eucharist. His body and blood become the sacrificial meal by which the community is able to share in the blessings and saving effects of his sacrifice. The Corinthians must learn to celebrate the Lord's Supper in a way that demonstrates how profoundly the Lord's sacrificial death has changed the conditions of people's relationships with one another and the responsibilities of people bound with God in covenant obligations.

In addition to repeating the words of Jesus, Paul adds his own understanding of the Eucharist: "For as often as you eat this bread and drink the cup, you proclaim the Lord's death until he comes" (v. 26). The sacrificial meal proclaims God's deliverance of his people through the death of Jesus and anticipates the fullness of God's salvation when Christ will come again in glory. It looks backward to the past and forward to the future, bringing Christ's past sacrifice and his future coming into the sacramental present of his church's liturgy.

Sharing the Lord's Supper "in an unworthy manner" (v. 27), in this context, means eating and drinking in a way that causes division, shows disregard for the poor and hungry, and forgets the obligations of the covenant. Self-centeredness, individualism, and arrogance make one "answerable for the body and blood of the Lord," that is, guilty of dishonoring the Eucharist. So, Christians who are preparing to share communion in Christ must "examine" themselves to make sure they are in a fit state to partake in the holy supper (verse 28). Those who eat and drink at the Eucharist "without discerning the body" eat and drink their own judgment (verse 29). Worthy communion means realizing the presence of the living Christ and the corporate unity of all who share his life.

REFLECTING

Consider what you are learning from Paul's message and how he challenges your membership in the body of Christ.

- The Greek words, translated as "received" and "handed on," are terms the rabbis of Paul's day used to describe the keeping and teaching of sacred tradition. Paul uses the same words when he hands on the teaching of Christ's death and resurrection (1 Corinthians 15:3). The truth about Christ's paschal mystery and the truth about the Eucharist were received from the Lord and handed on by the apostles. In what way are these two truths inseparable from each other and vital for the message of salvation Paul preached?

- After reminding his hearers of the eucharistic tradition that had been handed on to them, Paul says, "For as often as you eat this bread and drink the cup, you proclaim the Lord's death until he comes." In what way does the Eucharist bring the past and the future into a single graced moment?

PRAYING

After listening to God's word in Scripture, respond in prayer to God who always listens to your voice.

- Living Lord, through your apostles you have handed on the Eucharist to your church. You desire us to proclaim your saving death until you return in glory. Help me to examine myself and prepare for the eucharistic liturgy so that I will reflect your self-giving love for all people.

Continue examining yourself in silent prayer in order to receive the body and blood of Christ in a worthy manner.

ACTING

Consider ways you wish to put the teachings of Paul into practice for your discipleship.

- Paul says that Christians must first examine themselves before partaking in eucharistic communion. In consideration of what I have learned from Paul about the Eucharist, what are the kinds of questions I should ask myself as I prepare to participate in the Mass? How will I prepare myself for Mass this Sunday?

Section II

Honoring God in Covenant Worship

The church's eucharistic liturgy is indeed biblical worship. We could say that in the Mass the biblical history of salvation comes to its completion before our eyes. This history of God's relationship with his people can be summarized in the succession of covenants that God established, especially the covenants made with Abraham, Moses, David, and Jesus. Scripture presents these covenants as a dynamic unity, beginning with the call of Abraham and ending with the completed kingdom of God. In fact, from the perspective of God, there is only one covenant, which is the eternally valid covenant made with Abraham and perfectly fulfilled in Jesus Christ.

In the ancient Near East, covenantal rituals were like adoption ceremonies: they established kinship, symbolized by blood, between previously unrelated parties. In the biblical understanding, the covenant is not a mutual agreement between God and his people, but an unsought divine gift, a creative act of God's love. God established a sacred bond with the family of Abraham, offered him unconditional promises that would extend to all the nations, and ratified the covenant in blood sacrifices. Through Moses, the covenant was extended to the nation of Israel, instituted through the reciprocal obligations given on Mount Sinai, and established through offering the flesh of animals and sprinkling their blood upon the people. In covenant with David, God promised the Messiah from his lineage and established daily sacrifices at the temple for the remission of sin and reconciliation with God. In each period of history, God established a sacred bond of kinship with his people through the rituals of the covenant.

At the Last Supper, by declaring the cup to contain the "blood of the covenant," Jesus declared that his own blood, poured out in his Passion and made really present in the Eucharist, establishes the new and everlasting covenant, the eternal blood-union or bond of kinship between God and all who share the life of his Son. In the church's liturgy, the sacrificial offering of his flesh and blood on the cross is made present again, the covenant is renewed, and all who share in the sacred meal are united in his risen life.

In this section, we will look at the biblical roots of the eucharistic liturgy in order to understand it as the culmination of God's whole plan. It may seem surprising that so much of this foundation depends on Old Testament texts. Although the sacrifices of the law of Israel have been taken up into the perfect sacrifice of the new covenant, this does not reduce the importance of the Hebrew Scriptures. As St. Augustine taught, "the New Testament lies hidden in the Old and the Old is unveiled in the New."

Before looking at each part of the liturgy in later sections of this study, we first look at the Mass as a covenant liturgy, rooted in Israel and consisting of scriptural proclamation, sacrificial offering, and sacred meal. By tracing the foundations of Eucharist from Old Testament archetypes, to the mission of Jesus, to the ongoing sacramental life of his church, we will see the Mass as the culmination of God's saving plan for us.

- Why is the Old Testament so essential for understanding the church's liturgy?

- Why would God choose to relate to his people through covenant?

- What do I hope to understand more fully about the roots of the Mass?

Lesson 1

The Defining Drama
and Memorial Feast of Passover

Listening

From age to age, the people of Israel repeated this story and memorialized their redemption in this meal. Listen to this defining narrative as if you are hearing it with the wide-eyed fascination of a Jewish child.

Exodus 12:1–14

¹The LORD said to Moses and Aaron in the land of Egypt: ²This month shall mark for you the beginning of months; it shall be the first month of the year for you. ³Tell the whole congregation of Israel that on the tenth of this month they are to take a lamb for each family, a lamb for each household. ⁴If a household is too small for a whole lamb, it shall join its closest neighbor in obtaining one; the lamb shall be divided in proportion to the number of people who eat of it. ⁵Your lamb shall be without blemish, a year-old male; you may take it from the sheep or from the goats. ⁶You shall keep it until the fourteenth day of this month; then the whole assembled congregation of Israel shall slaughter it at twilight. ⁷They shall take some of the blood and put it on the two doorposts and the lintel of the houses in which they eat it. ⁸They shall eat the lamb that same night; they shall eat it roasted over the fire with unleavened bread and bitter herbs. ⁹Do not eat any of it raw or boiled in water, but roasted over the fire, with its head, legs, and inner organs. ¹⁰You shall let none of it remain until the morning; anything that remains until the morning you shall burn. ¹¹This is how you shall eat it: your loins girded, your sandals on your feet, and your staff in your hand; and you shall eat it hurriedly. It is the passover of the LORD. ¹²For I will pass through the land of Egypt that night, and I will strike down every firstborn in the land of Egypt, both human beings and animals; on all the gods of Egypt I will execute judgments: I

am the LORD. [13]The blood shall be a sign for you on the houses where you live: when I see the blood, I will pass over you, and no plague shall destroy you when I strike the land of Egypt.

[14]This day shall be a day of remembrance for you. You shall celebrate it as a festival to the LORD; throughout your generations you shall observe it as a perpetual ordinance.

UNDERSTANDING

Continue seeking to understand this text and its significance through the wisdom of the church's scholarship and tradition. Highlight or underline the phrases that seem most significant to you.

The first Passover came at the climax of God's actions to free the Israelites from slavery. Nine plagues of increasing severity had already befallen Egypt in order to convince Pharaoh to release the Israelites. The final and most terrible plague was the death of the firstborn in every family, from Pharaoh's son down to the firstborn of the animals. The Israelites would escape the plague because their houses would be marked by the redeeming blood of the sacrificed lamb. God told the Israelites, "When I see the blood, I will pass over you" (v. 13).

Throughout the book of Exodus, historical narrative and ritual instructions are woven together. Here the story of the first Passover pauses to introduce directives for commemorating the event in the years to come. When the Israelites of future generations reenacted the Passover, it became not simply a recollection of past events. Every time God's people memorialized the event of Passover throughout the centuries, the ritual made the saving power of the past event present again. Because of God's word and promise, the redeeming reality of the original Passover became real in the ritual's timeless moment. It is as though all the past and future generations of Israel came together around the Passover table to be reconstituted as the people of God.

The annual celebration of Passover consisted of two main parts: the slaying of the lamb in the temple of Jerusalem, followed by the eating of the lamb around the family table. This combination of the sacrificial death of the lamb and the eating of the lamb's flesh in a ritual meal is called a communion sacrifice in Israel's tradition. As the people ate the sacrificial lamb, they shared more intimately in the offering of the sacrifice and offered their lives to God in the offering of the lamb. Explained through the reading of Scripture and eaten with unleavened bread, bitter herbs, and cups of wine, the yearly rite became the means for all generations to celebrate their covenant with God, who saved them from slavery and death.

God commanded his people to observe Passover as "a perpetual ordinance." He told his people that the annual ritual would be a "remembrance" for them. Thousands of years after the exodus, Jewish parents would still explain the Passover ritual to their children: "It is because of what the LORD did for me when I came out of Egypt" (Exod 13:8). The meal became the personal connection of each generation back to the foundational events of their salvation.

At the time of Jesus, Passover was celebrated as a pilgrimage feast in which many Jews would travel to Jerusalem. Each gospel emphasizes that the final events of Jesus' life took place in the context of Passover. The gospels of Matthew, Mark, and Luke describe the Last Supper as a Passover meal that Jesus celebrated with his disciples at table on the night before his death. The gospel of John, however, places the crucifixion and death of Jesus at the same time as the Passover lambs were being sacrificed in Jerusalem's temple. For John, Jesus is truly the Lamb of God, the Lamb who fulfills the Passover sacrifices of old.

At the Last Supper, Jesus desired to institute a new Passover memorial, one that would remember the mighty act of salvation by which we are freed from sin and death. While the Passover of Israel interprets and memorializes the central event of the Old Testament (the exodus from bondage and freedom in the land), the Eucharist interprets and remembers the central event of the New Testament (Jesus' death and resurrection). Both remembrances were given on the evening before the historical event occurred, and both serve to connect subsequent generations to that redeeming experience.

REFLECTING

Try to find ways to personalize this text, realizing that all Scripture is inspired and able to teach God's truth. These suggestions will help apply the text to the context of your life.

- In the story of Abraham preparing to sacrifice his beloved son, the young Isaac asked his father, "Where is the lamb for the sacrifice?" Abraham said to his son, "God himself will provide the lamb" (Gen 22:7–8). How has God continually provided a lamb for the sacrifices of his people?

- In a letter to the Corinthians, Paul proclaims, "Our paschal lamb, Christ, has been sacrificed" (1 Cor 5:7). In what way does a study of Exodus help me understand the meaning of Paul's announcement? In what ways does the Passion and death of Jesus fulfill the ancient Passover?

- The Passover consists of a sacrificial offering and a sacrificial meal. What are some of the parallels and connections between the annual Jewish Passover and the eucharistic liturgy of Christians?

PRAYING

Pray to God in response to the divine word spoken to you in the Scriptures.

- Saving God, you revealed your compassionate presence to the people of Israel by freeing them from bondage and calling them to new life. I claim the freedom from sin and death that you have given to me through your Son, Jesus Christ. Renew my spirit today through the power of your word and through your amazing forgiveness.

Continue praying that your heart may find new freedom to confess Jesus as Lord and to be renewed in his life.

ACTING

Realize that God's word has the power to change your heart and rearrange your life.

- As the Passover of Israel made present the exodus from Egypt for each participant, the eucharistic liturgy makes present the life-giving death and resurrection of Jesus. How can I live today fully conscious that I am a baptized Christian, aware that I have been freed from the effects of sin, death, and meaningless existence? What difference does it make when I live consciously in light of the new life I possess in the risen Lord?

LESSON 2

The Book of the Covenant and the Blood of Sacrifice

LISTENING

Prepare for these moments by closing off the distractions of the day and entering a space where you can listen to the scriptural text with focused attention. Listen carefully like the people of Israel who listened to Moses read from the book of the covenant.

Exodus 24:1–11

¹Then [God] said to Moses, "Come up to the LORD, you and Aaron, Nadab, and Abihu, and seventy of the elders of Israel, and worship at a distance. ²Moses alone shall come near the LORD; but the others shall not come near, and the people shall not come up with him."

³Moses came and told the people all the words of the LORD and all the ordinances; and all the people answered with one voice, and said, "All the words that the LORD has spoken we will do." ⁴And Moses wrote down all the words of the LORD. He rose early in the morning, and built an altar at the foot of the mountain, and set up twelve pillars, corresponding to the twelve tribes of Israel. ⁵He sent young men of the people of Israel, who offered burnt offerings and sacrificed oxen as offerings of well-being to the LORD. ⁶Moses took half of the blood and put it in basins, and half of the blood he dashed against the altar. ⁷Then he took the book of the covenant, and read it in the hearing of the people; and they said, "All that the LORD has spoken we will do, and we will be obedient." ⁸Moses took the blood and dashed it on the people, and said, "See the blood of the covenant that the LORD has made with you in accordance with all these words."

⁹Then Moses and Aaron, Nadab, and Abihu, and seventy of the elders of Israel went up, ¹⁰and they saw the God of Israel. Under his feet there was something like a pavement of sapphire stone, like the very heaven for clearness. ¹¹God did not lay his hand on the chief men of the people of Israel; also they beheld God, and they ate and drank.

Hebrews 9:15–22

¹⁵For this reason [Christ] is the mediator of a new covenant, so that those who are called may receive the promised eternal inheritance, because a death has occurred that redeems them from the transgressions under the first covenant. ¹⁶Where a will is involved, the death of the one who made it must be established. ¹⁷For a will takes effect only at death, since it is not in force as long as the one who made it is alive. ¹⁸Hence not even the first covenant was inaugurated without blood. ¹⁹For when every commandment had been told to all the people by Moses in accordance with the law, he took the blood of calves and goats, with water and scarlet wool and hyssop, and sprinkled both the scroll itself and all the people, ²⁰saying, "This is the blood of the covenant that God has ordained for you." ²¹And in the same way he sprinkled with the blood both the tent and all the vessels used in worship. ²²Indeed, under the law almost everything is purified with blood, and without the shedding of blood there is no forgiveness of sins.

UNDERSTANDING

Continue to explore the meaning of the ancient sacrifice and the sprinkling of blood in order to understand how the old covenant is fulfilled in the new.

The pledge of covenant is found throughout the Old Testament, describing the unique relationship between God and his people. At Mount Sinai, God established a covenant with the Israelites that would forever define their history as a people. The Israelites were assured of God's blessings, and they promised to obey his word and live as a priestly people.

The solemn ceremonies that accompanied the making of the covenant emphasize its seriousness and permanence. Moses wrote down the words and ordinances of God in a "book of the covenant." He then built an altar and sealed the covenant with the blood of sacrifice. He dashed half of the blood of the sacrificed animals upon the altar, representing God. Then, after Moses read the book of the covenant and the people vowed to live according to the words of the book, he dashed the other half of the blood upon the people. The blood is the seal and pledge of the covenant, establishing a community of life between God and his people. This blood bond is described by Moses as "the blood of the covenant that the LORD has made with you" (v. 8). Following this, Moses and the elders ate a sacrificial meal in the presence of God (v. 11).

Though renewals of Israel's covenant with God are recorded throughout the Scriptures at critical junctures in history, God's people often broke the covenant. Yet, despite their infidelity, God remained faithful and promised to establish a "new covenant" with them in the coming age. The prophet Jeremiah foresaw a new covenant that would be written on the heart and not on stone tablets as at Sinai; it would be a relationship based on internal conviction rather than external obligation. In this new relationship, God's people would all know him and experience forgiveness of their sins (Jer 31:33–34).

The new covenant in Jesus Christ required both his death and the shedding of his blood. To explain the significance of Christ's death, the author of Hebrews shows that the Greek word for covenant can also mean "will" or "testament." Like a last will and testament, the covenant only takes effect when the person making the will dies (vv. 15–17). The death of Jesus was the way we received "the promised eternal inheritance."

The author of Hebrews also explains how the covenant with Moses was established with "the blood of the covenant" (vv. 18–22). The scroll of the law, the holy place, the vessels of worship, and God's people were sprinkled with the sacrificial blood. The author clarifies, "Under the law almost everything is purified with blood, and without the shedding of blood there is no forgiveness of sins." Thus the new covenant was established with the death of Christ and the shedding of his blood, the eternal sacrifice on the cross and the blood of the covenant.

The gospel accounts of the Last Supper demonstrate how Jesus established the ritual of the new covenant that was consummated on the cross through his sacrificial love. Jesus said, "This is my body which is given for you," and, "This cup that is poured out for you is the new covenant in my blood" (Luke 22:19–20). In celebrating the eucharistic liturgy, the church joins itself with the sacrifice of Christ, his self-giving death on the cross, and the Father's acceptance of the sacrifice in Christ's resurrection to life. The sacrificed body of Christ and the shed blood of Christ, made present again on the altar and given to his people to eat and drink, is the renewal of the new and everlasting covenant.

REFLECTING

Spend some time reflecting on the implications of these biblical texts for your own life, then write out your responses to these questions:

- In the covenant ceremony on Mount Sinai, Moses read from God's word in the book and then dashed the blood of the sacrificial offering on the people. What are some of the parallels between this ancient covenant ritual and the Christian eucharistic liturgy?

- Moses dashed the sacrificial blood on the altar and then on the people. What is the significance of the blood in the ritual of sacrifice? What does the blood on the altar and the blood on the people express to me about the significance of the covenant?

- In all covenant ritual, blood is vital for the establishment of the kinship bond. What are some of the differences between the terms of the ancient Sinai covenant and the new covenant in Christ? In what ways are these differences expressed through the covenant rituals of each?

PRAYING

Respond to your listening to God's word in the words of prayer.

- God of the covenant, on the mountain at Sinai you bound yourself forever to your people, and you renewed your covenant with them throughout ancient history. As I listen to your word in Scripture, teach me your ways and help me understand the promises you offer to me. Help me to respond to the words of your covenant with obedience and carry out all you have spoken to me.

Continue praying with trust and confidence in God's covenant promises. When words no longer seem necessary, just rest in the presence of our faithful God.

ACTING

Consider your unity in God's word with God's covenanted people throughout history.

- After Moses read the book of the covenant in the hearing of the people, they replied, "All that the LORD has spoken we will do, and we will be obedient." In what way am I called today to respond in obedience to the word of God in Scripture?

LESSON 3

Sacrifice Offered for the Atonement of Sin

LISTENING

Listen for the parallels and differences between the old covenant text and the new. As you read, highlight or underline passages that seem most pertinent to you. These marks will help you recall your experience of hearing the sacred texts and seeking to understand their significance.

Leviticus 16:1–16

¹The LORD spoke to Moses after the death of the two sons of Aaron, when they drew near before the LORD and died. ²The LORD said to Moses: Tell your brother Aaron not to come just at any time into the sanctuary inside the curtain before the mercy seat that is upon the ark, or he will die; for I appear in the cloud upon the mercy seat. ³Thus shall Aaron come into the holy place: with a young bull for a sin offering and a ram for a burnt offering. ⁴He shall put on the holy linen tunic, and shall have the linen undergarments next to his body, fasten the linen sash, and wear the linen turban; these are the holy vestments. He shall bathe his body in water, and then put them on. ⁵He shall take from the congregation of the people of Israel two male goats for a sin offering, and one ram for a burnt offering.

⁶Aaron shall offer the bull as a sin offering for himself, and shall make atonement for himself and for his house. ⁷He shall take the two goats and set them before the LORD at the entrance of the tent of meeting; ⁸and Aaron shall cast lots on the two goats, one lot for the LORD and the other lot for Azazel. ⁹Aaron shall present the goat on which the lot fell for the LORD, and offer it as a sin offering; ¹⁰but the goat on which the lot fell for Azazel shall be presented alive before the LORD to make atonement over it, that it may be sent away into the wilderness to Azazel.

¹¹Aaron shall present the bull as a sin offering for himself, and shall make atonement for himself and for his house; he shall slaughter the bull as a sin offering for himself. ¹²He shall take a censer full of coals of fire from the altar before the LORD, and two handfuls of crushed sweet incense, and he shall bring it inside the curtain ¹³and put the incense on the fire before the LORD, that the cloud of the incense may cover the mercy seat that is upon the covenant, or he will die. ¹⁴He shall take some of the blood of the bull, and sprinkle it with his finger on the front of the mercy seat, and before the mercy seat he shall sprinkle the blood with his finger seven times.

¹⁵He shall slaughter the goat of the sin offering that is for the people and bring its blood inside the curtain, and do with its blood as he did with the blood of the bull, sprinkling it upon the mercy seat and before the mercy seat. ¹⁶Thus he shall make atonement for the sanctuary, because of the uncleannesses of the people of Israel, and because of their transgressions, all their sins; and so he shall do for the tent of meeting, which remains with them in the midst of their uncleannesses.

Hebrews 9:11–14, 23–28

¹¹But when Christ came as a high priest of the good things that have come, then through the greater and perfect tent (not made with hands, that is, not of this creation), ¹²he entered once for all into the Holy Place, not with the blood of goats and calves, but with his own blood, thus obtaining eternal redemption. ¹³For if the blood of goats and bulls, with the sprinkling of the ashes of a heifer, sanctifies those who have been defiled so that their flesh is purified, ¹⁴how much more will the blood of Christ, who through the eternal Spirit offered himself without blemish to God, purify our conscience from dead works to worship the living God!

²³Thus it was necessary for the sketches of the heavenly things to be purified with these rites, but the heavenly things themselves need better sacrifices than these. ²⁴For Christ did not enter a sanctuary made by human hands, a mere copy of the true one, but he entered into heaven itself, now to appear in the presence of God on our behalf. ²⁵Nor was it to offer himself again and again, as the high priest enters the Holy Place year after year with blood that is not his own; ²⁶for then he would have had to suffer again and again since the foundation of the world. But as it is, he has appeared once for all at the end of the age to remove sin by the sacrifice of himself. ²⁷And just as it is appointed for mortals to die once, and after that the judgment, ²⁸so Christ, having been offered once to bear the sins of many, will appear a second time, not to deal with sin, but to save those who are eagerly waiting for him.

UNDERSTANDING

Continue searching for the meaning and significance of these two texts. Mark up the text as you make discoveries and find new insights.

Offering sacrifice was a universal practice in the religions of the ancient world, and it is at the core of the religious devotion and practice found in the Bible. Biblical worship is essentially the offering of sacrifice. Generally speaking, to sacrifice is to make an offering to God of something of value — an animal, grain, food, drink, or incense. This offering can have many meanings, but underlying every sacrificial act is a recognition of the debt we owe to God as the source of life and blessing.

In Israel, as in most of the ancient world, blood was considered sacred because it is the bearer of life. The release of blood was understood as the release of life, and in sacrifice the respectful slaughter of the animal with the shedding of blood expressed the surrender of a life to God. The blood was poured on the altar (Lev 1:5), placed on the doorframe of the houses (Exod 12:7), sprinkled upon the assembly (Exod 24:8), or sprinkled upon the mercy seat above the ark of the covenant (Lev 16:14–15).

In a sin offering or burnt offering, the life of the animal victim substituted for the life of the sinful person. The one offering the sacrifice symbolically offered his or her own life to God, reestablishing the relationship with God. As God said in the book of Leviticus: "For the life of the flesh is in the blood; and I have given it to you for making atonement for your lives on the altar; for, as life, it is the blood that makes atonement" (Lev 17:11).

The most important communal sacrifices were the offering of the bull, the ram, and the goat on the annual Day of Atonement. On this one day of the year, the high priest entered the inner sanctum of Jerusalem's temple with a censer of hot coals and incense and the blood of the sacrificed animals. After engulfing the sanctuary with the haze of incense, the high priest sprinkled the blood on the mercy seat where God was known to dwell. In this way, he made atonement for his own sins and brought reconciliation between the Israelites and God.

Every type of sacrifice in the Old Testament prefigures a different effect of Christ's redeeming sacrifice. God's people under the old covenant were waiting and hoping, reaching forward toward an experience of God they could not yet grasp. They worshiped God in a transitory sanctuary, offering imperfect sacrifices through a provisional priesthood. The temple and all its rituals were shadows, "sketches" (Heb 9:23), or "copies" (Heb 9:24), preparing for "the good things that have come" (Heb 9:11) through the new covenant in Christ. The ancient Torah points from within itself to beyond itself. This new covenant brought an end to the bloody sacrifices of the old law through "the precious blood of Christ" (1 Pet 1:19). For Paul, the offering of Christ on the cross is "a sacrifice of atonement by his blood" (Rom 3:25).

Every type of sacrifice under the old covenant was fulfilled in Christ. While the gospels depict the death of Jesus as a fulfillment of the Passover sacrifice, Hebrews focuses on the sacrifices of the Day of Atonement. Here we see Jesus not as the slain Lamb, but as the high priest who bears the atoning sacrifice of his own blood into the heavenly presence of God (Heb 9:11–12). Christ, as the final and perfect high priest, "has appeared once for all at the end of the age to remove sin by the sacrifice of himself" (Heb 9:26). In him we can enter into an intimate encounter with God, personally know his loving forgiveness, and truly worship the living God.

Our worship of God in the eucharistic liturgy is a form of sacrificial offering. It is, as described in Hebrews, a cosmic Day of Atonement. Jesus the high priest truly offers his own life and blood to the Father. Yet, unlike the sacrifices of the old covenant, Christ's sacrifice was a once-and-for-all sacrifice, adequate for all time (Heb 9:12, 25–26). Christ does not die and shed his blood again at every eucharistic liturgy, but at every Mass we participate in his one sacrifice and join ourselves to his holy and perfect offering to the Father.

REFLECTING

Let the ancient rituals given by God to Israel interact with your own experiences of unworthiness, sin, fear, and hope. Consider how the sacrifice of Christ brings about a completion and satisfaction of your longings.

- How does the ritual of the Day of Atonement express God's desire for a right relationship with his people? Why was this ritual of reconciliation so important for the Israelites?

- Leviticus says that "the life of the flesh is in the blood." What was done with the blood of the sacrificial victim in the old covenant sacrifices? How do these ancient sacrifices help me understand the atonement and reconciliation offered to me through Christ's Eucharist?

- If Christ died "once for all," then what is the connection between Christ's sacrificial offering to the Father in heaven and the sacrifice of the Mass?

PRAYING

Offer your prayer to God in response to your understanding of his word in Scripture.

- Faithful God, the blood of the ancient sacrifices expresses the serious rupture of human sin and the crucial importance of atonement with you. Reconcile me through the precious blood of Christ so that I may forever give you praise and worship.

Continue praying with trusting confidence to God, who has reconciled you to himself through the sacrifice of Jesus Christ. Rest in gratitude that you are able to approach God without fear and trembling.

ACTING

Consider the practical implications of the fact that we are made one with God through the atonement sacrifice of Christ.

- Though Christ offered his blood only once for all people on the cross, he gave us an everlasting memorial through which we can continue to participate in his one sacrifice and receive the gift of his saving grace. In what way do I experience the Mass as an intimate encounter of atonement with God? How can I receive this reconciling grace more confidently?

LESSON 4

A Thanksgiving Offering for Deliverance

LISTENING

Listen to these ancient texts, letting God give you new insights as you approach the inspired page with your own pains, fears, hope, and gratitude.

Leviticus 7:11–15

¹¹This is the ritual of the sacrifice of the offering of well-being that one may offer to the LORD. ¹²If you offer it for thanksgiving, you shall offer with the thank offering unleavened cakes mixed with oil, unleavened wafers spread with oil, and cakes of choice flour well soaked in oil. ¹³With your thanksgiving sacrifice of well-being you shall bring your offering with cakes of leavened bread. ¹⁴From this you shall offer one cake from each offering, as a gift to the LORD; it shall belong to the priest who dashes the blood of the offering of well-being. ¹⁵And the flesh of your thanksgiving sacrifice of well-being shall be eaten on the day it is offered; you shall not leave any of it until morning.

Psalm 116:1–19

¹I love the LORD, because he has heard
   my voice and my supplications.
²Because he inclined his ear to me,
   therefore I will call on him as long as I live.
³The snares of death encompassed me;
   the pangs of Sheol laid hold on me;
   I suffered distress and anguish.
⁴Then I called on the name of the LORD:
   "O LORD, I pray, save my life!"

⁵Gracious is the Lord, and righteous;
    our God is merciful.
⁶The Lord protects the simple;
    when I was brought low, he saved me.
⁷Return, O my soul, to your rest,
    for the Lord has dealt bountifully with you.

⁸For you have delivered my soul from death,
    my eyes from tears,
    my feet from stumbling.
⁹I walk before the Lord
    in the land of the living.
¹⁰I kept my faith, even when I said,
    "I am greatly afflicted";
¹¹I said in my consternation,
    "Everyone is a liar."

¹²What shall I return to the Lord
    for all his bounty to me?
¹³I will lift up the cup of salvation
    and call on the name of the Lord,
¹⁴I will pay my vows to the Lord
    in the presence of all his people.
¹⁵Precious in the sight of the Lord
    is the death of his faithful ones.
¹⁶O Lord, I am your servant;
    I am your servant, the child of your serving girl.
    You have loosed my bonds.
¹⁷I will offer to you a thanksgiving sacrifice
    and call on the name of the Lord.
¹⁸I will pay my vows to the Lord
    in the presence of all his people,
¹⁹in the courts of the house of the Lord,
    in your midst, O Jerusalem.
Praise the Lord!

Understanding

Continue searching for the meaning and significance of these texts as you consider the ways that the Israelites expressed gratitude to God for deliverance from evil and death.

Among the many types of sacrifices under God's covenant with Moses was the offering of thanksgiving (in Hebrew *todah*, in Greek *eucharistia*). This liturgical ritual was performed by one who had experienced God's deliverance from a great trial or mortal danger. Leviticus specifies that the one rescued expresses public acclamation of God's saving action with a sacrifice in the temple, including unleavened cakes and wafers, followed by a thanksgiving meal with family and friends in which the sacrificed victim was consumed along with the consecrated bread.

The thanksgiving ritual was accompanied by a sung narrative, usually in the form of a psalm. The structure of these songs usually moved from lament to praise. The psalm first expressed the circumstances of pending death, then a cry to God for deliverance, followed by the rescue from death by God, and finally, thanksgiving for God's redeeming goodness. Psalm 116 expresses these elements: danger and distress (v. 3), plea for deliverance (v. 4), God's merciful response (vv. 5–9), and a ritual of gratitude (vv. 12–19). This public liturgy includes lifting up "the cup of salvation" and offering "a thanksgiving sacrifice," both performed while calling on "the name of the LORD."

The Passover of Israel took the form of a collective thanksgiving sacrifice, including the sacrificed lamb, unleavened bread and wine, and narrative prayers and psalms. The Israelites lamented their oppressive enslavement, cried out to God for deliverance, were redeemed by God in the exodus, and proclaimed God's salvation with thanksgiving and praise in the Passover sacrificial offering and meal. The Hallel psalms sung at Passover included Psalm 116, incorporating the lament and thanksgiving of individuals into the corporate liturgy of the nation.

As the psalms and prophets of Israel expressed Israel's thanksgiving ritual, they conveyed a growing understanding that God required more than animal sacrifices offered on the altar. God desired an interior or spiritual sacrifice as well. The sacrifices the Israelites offered in the temple were to reflect their offering of themselves with a contrite and humble spirit to do God's will. In fact, a lack of faith and justice could make an offering in the temple worthless before God. Over time, Israel came to see that love, not sacrifice, is what God desires most.

The ancient rabbis believed that when the Messiah would come, all offerings except the thanksgiving (todah) sacrifice would cease, and the thank offering would continue for all eternity. When the temple of Jerusalem was destroyed in AD 70, all of the bloody animal sacrifices stopped. Only the thanksgiving (eucharistia) sacrifice remained, the Eucharist of Christ's church.

The self-offering of Christ and its remembrance in the eucharistic liturgy of the church completes all the sacrificial rituals of ancient Israel. The sin offerings, the Day of Atonement liturgy, the Passover sacrifice and meal, and the thanksgiving sacrifices are fulfilled in the Christian Eucharist. With the temple's destruction after the redemption of the Messiah, the eucharistic sacrifice outlasted all other sacrifices and continued throughout the ages.

Though Jesus celebrated the Last Supper in the context of Israel's Passover, he reconfigured it around his own self-sacrifice in a way that more perfectly expresses its nature as a thanksgiving sacrifice. Jesus took the bread and wine and gave "thanks" (*eucharistia*) over them (Luke 22:19). Unlike the once-a-year celebration of Passover, the thanksgiving sacrifice could be offered at any time. This model permitted weekly and even daily celebration of the Christian Eucharist.

The Eucharist is the thanksgiving (*todah*) offering of the Risen Christ. Its narrative is his passion, death, and resurrection, exemplifying the movement from lament to grateful praise. As his body, the church offers up its trials and tribulations in union with the sacrifice of Christ. The background of Israel's thanksgiving sacrifice demonstrates how the Eucharist is both a proclamation of the Lord's death (1 Cor 11:26) and an expression of praise and thanks to God for the deliverance he has brought to us in Christ.

REFLECTING

Spend some time reflecting on the thanksgiving sacrifice of Israel in relationship to your understanding of Eucharist. Let the ancient text interact with your own memories, hopes, suffering, and gratitude.

- The thanksgiving sacrifice of Israel forms the ancient context for the eucharistic liturgy. What are some of the similarities and parallels between these sacred rituals?

- The Eucharist is the thanksgiving offering of the risen Christ. In what ways does this understanding deepen my appreciation of the Mass?

- God allows trials and tribulations in our lives so that we can learn to offer them as sacrifice to God with Christ. How can I learn to offer up my prayers, works, joys, and sufferings in union with the holy sacrifice of the Mass?

PRAYING

Psalm 22, which Jesus prayed on the cross, is one of the many psalms sung in the context of Israel's thanksgiving sacrifices. Beginning with a cry of dereliction ("My God, my God, why have You forsaken me?"), it recounts torments at the hands of evildoers and concludes on a note of triumphant praise.

- Read or chant this psalm through him, with him, and in him. Move with Christ in prayer from suffering and lament to joyful praise and gratitude for God's deliverance.

Allow this psalm to lead you to your own prayer of thanksgiving to God.

ACTING

Consider the practical implications of your understanding of Israel's thanksgiving sacrifice and Christian Eucharist.

- A deep sense of thankfulness leads to worship. When we cease to nurture gratitude, our worship withers. What practices would help me develop a deeper spirit of thankfulness and thus deepen my desire to worship God in Eucharist?

Encountering the Risen Christ in Word and Sacrament

Listening

Kiss the gospel text as a sign of honor to God's word within it. Allow your heart to burn within you like the hearts of the disciples on the road as the Risen Christ opened the Scriptures to them.

Luke 24:13–35

¹³Now on that same day two of them were going to a village called Emmaus, about seven miles from Jerusalem, ¹⁴and talking with each other about all these things that had happened. ¹⁵While they were talking and discussing, Jesus himself came near and went with them, ¹⁶but their eyes were kept from recognizing him. ¹⁷And he said to them, "What are you discussing with each other while you walk along?" They stood still, looking sad. ¹⁸Then one of them, whose name was Cleopas, answered him, "Are you the only stranger in Jerusalem who does not know the things that have taken place there in these days?" ¹⁹He asked them, "What things?" They replied, "The things about Jesus of Nazareth, who was a prophet mighty in deed and word before God and all the people, ²⁰and how our chief priests and leaders handed him over to be condemned to death and crucified him. ²¹But we had hoped that he was the one to redeem Israel. Yes, and besides all this, it is now the third day since these things took place. ²²Moreover, some women of our group astounded us. They were at the tomb early this morning, ²³and when they did not find his body there, they came back and told us that they had indeed seen a vision of angels who said that he was alive. ²⁴Some of those who were with us went to the tomb and found it just as the women had said; but they did not see him." ²⁵Then he said to them, "Oh, how foolish you are, and how slow of heart to believe all that the prophets have declared! ²⁶Was it not necessary that the Messiah should suffer these things and then enter into his

glory?" [27]Then beginning with Moses and all the prophets, he interpreted to them the things about himself in all the scriptures.

[28]As they came near the village to which they were going, he walked ahead as if he were going on. [29]But they urged him strongly, saying, "Stay with us, because it is almost evening and the day is now nearly over." So he went in to stay with them. [30]When he was at the table with them, he took bread, blessed and broke it, and gave it to them. [31]Then their eyes were opened, and they recognized him; and he vanished from their sight. [32]They said to each other, "Were not our hearts burning within us while he was talking to us on the road, while he was opening the scriptures to us?" [33]That same hour they got up and returned to Jerusalem; and they found the eleven and their companions gathered together. [34]They were saying, "The Lord has risen indeed, and he has appeared to Simon!" [35]Then they told what had happened on the road, and how he had been made known to them in the breaking of the bread.

UNDERSTANDING

After carefully reading the Scripture, continue searching for the significance of the text for your understanding of the eucharistic liturgy.

The walk to Emmaus took place "on that same day" (v. 13), that is, the first day of the week, the day of the resurrection. This is the day of the week on which the early Christians gathered for Eucharist. The fact that the two disciples were unknown outside of this text — Cleophas is only mentioned here and the other remains anonymous — points to the fact that this encounter with Christ could have occurred with any of his followers, not just the well-known apostles. And the fact that Emmaus was an unknown village, the location of which is still disputed today, emphasizes the point that this appearance occurred with ordinary, small-town folk.

We can assume that the two travelers were returning home from their Passover pilgrimage to Jerusalem, during which they experienced the heart-rending crucifixion of Jesus. Not surprisingly, they were talking about everything that happened (v. 14) — Jesus' torturous death, their shattered hopes, and the women's report of the empty tomb. When Jesus came up to them, he must have seemed like another pilgrim returning home (v. 15). Cleophas' question to him assumes that the crucifixion of Jesus was the talk of Jerusalem during the feast (verse 18). Ironically, it is Cleophas and his companion who do "not know the things that have taken place there in these days."

The response of Jesus is surprisingly forceful, especially as he reproaches them for not taking the Scriptures seriously regarding the suffering and glorification of the

Messiah (vv. 25–26). Jesus' interpretation of the Scriptures does not seem to refer to any singular passage. Rather, he laid out for them the way in which "all the scriptures" had led up to God's revelation of the cross and resurrection of Christ, "beginning with Moses and all the prophets" (v. 27). What an experience of the inspired word that must have been, as the risen Lord "interpreted" the Scriptures for them!

As evening descended and the day of resurrection was nearly over, the two disciples convince Jesus to stay with them (v. 29). Reclining at the table at the time of the evening meal, the guest became the host. When Jesus "took bread, blessed and broke it, and gave it" to the disciples, they recognized him (vv. 30–31). His gestures look back to his actions at the Last Supper and ahead to "the breaking of the bread" in Luke's description of the early church in Acts.

The Emmaus account was written with the experience of celebrating Christian worship in mind. The account helps Luke's readers to understand how the resurrected Lord is present to his church. Both the interpretation of the Scriptures and the breaking of the bread are actions of the risen Christ in which his presence is made real for the church. The account demonstrates the twofold structure of the Christian assembly and the dynamic relationship between word and sacrament.

As the narrative reaches its climax and Jesus vanishes from their sight, the disciples realize that it was Jesus they were experiencing all along. As "their eyes were opened, and they recognized him" (v. 31), they remembered that their hearts were burning with insight and love as Jesus interpreted the Scriptures for them (v. 32). Only after understanding the Scriptures are they prepared to recognize Jesus in the breaking of the bread and understand how "he had been made known to them" in intimate communion.

REFLECTING

Consider what this passage of the encounter with Jesus at Emmaus is showing you in the context of your weekly experience of the eucharistic liturgy.

- Jesus interpreted for the disciples at Emmaus the things about himself in all the Scriptures, "beginning with Moses and all the prophets." What does this experience of the disciples tell me about the significance of proclaiming the Scriptures in the church's liturgy?

- In this early description of the church's life, we see that the Lord's Risen presence is manifested in the Liturgy of the Word and the Liturgy of the Eucharist. What does this passage teach me about the intrinsic connection between word and sacrament, the Bible and liturgy?

- The disciples at Emmaus recognized Jesus in the breaking of the bread. In what sense were their eyes opened? In what sense were their hearts burning?

PRAYING

Let your listening and understanding now flow over into prayer.

- Glorified Christ, open the Scriptures to me, so that you may also open my eyes, mind, and heart to you. Assure me of your presence when I listen to Scripture and prepare me to recognize and know you in the celebration of the church's Eucharist.

Continue praying for the gift of deeper faith in the living presence of Christ in the eucharistic liturgy.

ACTING

The experience on the road with Jesus led the disciples to table with him. Then their experience of him at table led them back to the road to tell the good news of their encounter to others.

- How does the church's liturgy lead me from word to worship, then from worship to witness? What is one thing I could do to deepen my experience of Christ in word, worship, and witness?

LESSON 6

Worshiping the Lamb in Heaven's Liturgy

LISTENING

Hear the words of John as he describes the heavenly visions he is given on the Lord's day. Ask the Holy Spirit to guide your reading so that you grow to understand the inspired truth that God wishes you to understand from this text.

Revelation 5:6–14

⁶Then I saw between the throne and the four living creatures and among the elders a Lamb standing as if it had been slaughtered, having seven horns and seven eyes, which are the seven spirits of God sent out into all the earth. ⁷He went and took the scroll from the right hand of the one who was seated on the throne. ⁸When he had taken the scroll, the four living creatures and the twenty-four elders fell before the Lamb, each holding a harp and golden bowls full of incense, which are the prayers of the saints. ⁹They sing a new song:

"You are worthy to take the scroll
    and to open its seals,
for you were slaughtered and by your blood you ransomed for God
    saints from every tribe and language and people and nation;
¹⁰you have made them to be a kingdom and priests serving our God,
    and they will reign on earth."

¹¹Then I looked, and I heard the voice of many angels surrounding the throne and the living creatures and the elders; they numbered myriads of myriads and thousands of thousands, ¹²singing with full voice,

"Worthy is the Lamb that was slaughtered
to receive power and wealth and wisdom and might
and honor and glory and blessing!"

¹³Then I heard every creature in heaven and on earth and under the earth and in the sea, and all that is in them, singing,

> "To the one seated on the throne and to the Lamb
> be blessing and honor and glory and might forever and ever!"

¹⁴And the four living creatures said, "Amen!" And the elders fell down and worshiped.

UNDERSTANDING

Like much of Scripture, the book of Revelation is a liturgical text. Search for the understanding of the church's liturgy that you can learn from this passage.

John, the visionary of the book of Revelation, is granted "on the Lord's day" a series of visions of divine realities that were normally beyond human sight (1:9–11). He could have been celebrating the Christian Eucharist when he experienced this revelation. He was told to write down the visions and send the scroll to the seven churches to be read in their eucharistic assemblies. Through his writing, he takes us beyond our earthly experience to contemplate the eternal realities of heaven.

John sees a Lamb standing before the throne of God. Though it is evident that the Lamb has been put to death in sacrifice, it is now standing alive before the throne of God (v. 6). The Lamb is the crucified and risen Christ, the Lamb of God, whom all the lambs of sacrifice in the Old Testament prefigured. He is upright because "standing" is the ancient Christian posture of the resurrection and the posture of Israelite priests in offering sacrificial worship. But at the same time he is showing the Father his wounds, presenting the fact that he has died and given his life in exchange for the life of the world. Since seven represents divine completion, the Lamb's seven horns and seven eyes express his divine power and divine knowledge. The seven spirits of God reveal that God's Lamb possesses the Holy Spirit and sends that Spirit to all people.

This vision of John is the timeless sacrifice of Jesus being offered eternally to the Father. It is the constant worship of God in the heavenly liturgy in which the angels and saints and all creation participate. The blood of the Lamb is the offering that surpasses all others, the one sacrifice that makes people of every language and nation "a kingdom and priests serving our God (v. 9). In relationship to God, the Lamb is the perfect priest offering himself in sacrifice. In relationship to us, he is the atonement for our sins and the source of new and eternal life.

Whenever we celebrate the eucharistic liturgy of the church on earth, we become part of the eternal adoration John describes in his vision. We worship God together with people throughout the world, united with all the creatures of heaven enjoying the fullness of God's presence. What John was able to glimpse directly is still veiled from our eyes, though it is no less real for us. Every Eucharist, no matter how humble the church building or how obscure the location, has a universal character. It unites earth and heaven, creatures both visible and invisible, embracing all of creation. The church's liturgy is the experience of heaven on earth and a real participation in the life we hope to live forever.

The book of Revelation was written in the context of the eucharistic liturgy of the early Christians, and the book has influenced the development of that liturgy through the ages. In the book of Revelation we see vested priests, an altar, lampstands, and the smoke of incense. We hear a congregation chanting "holy, holy, holy" and singing "Amen" and "Alleluia." We experience the words and actions of sacrificial worship. The worship of God in the book of Revelation is the worship God's people offer to God in the Mass.

The book of Revelation is appropriately placed as the last book of the Bible because in it we see the culmination of biblical history. Likewise, every time we celebrate Eucharist, we are experiencing the completion of all God was accomplishing through the history of salvation. The Bible concludes with the Lord's promise, "I am coming soon," and with the liturgical cry of his church, "Amen, Come, Lord Jesus!" (Rev 22:20). Though this surely refers to Christ's return at the end of time, it also reflects the reality that Christ comes to us every time we celebrate the divine liturgy. Where the Bible leaves off, the Mass begins. As his church prays for his coming with liturgical cries and acclamation, Christ truly comes to us and we participate in his eternal worship of the Father.

REFLECTING

Spend some time reflecting on the Scripture in terms of your own discipleship. After meditating on the questions, write out your answers to each:

- When we celebrate the Mass, we do God's will most fully "on earth as it is in heaven." In what sense does this understanding of the Eucharist, as heaven on earth, add to my understanding and appreciation of the church's worship?

- The book of Revelation expresses the completion of God's saving plan through liturgical images and symbols. In what sense does the Bible lead to the Mass?

- John's vision shows the timeless sacrifice of Jesus being offered eternally to the Father. How does this image demonstrate that the Mass is not a new sacrifice of Christ but rather a participation in Christ's once-for-all sacrifice on the cross?

PRAYING

Speak to God in response to the words, ideas, and images of your listening and reflecting.

- Eternal Priest and perfect sacrifice, you are worthy to receive blessing, honor, power, and glory forever. Thank you for the great gift of allowing me to share in your timeless sacrifice to the Father through the gift of the Eucharist.

Continue saying or chanting repeatedly, "Come, Lord Jesus."

ACTING

As people who share in the Eucharist, we take on the task of building a world more in harmony with God's plan, so that God's will might be done on earth as it is in heaven.

- What can I do this week to promote solidarity and justice in the church and in the world, so that through God's grace and our cooperation, the earth might reflect the heavenly communion of all God's creatures?

Group Session Guide for Section II

Begin with hospitality and welcome. Offer any announcements or instructions before entering the spirit of focused discussion. Discuss these questions or those of your own choosing:

1. What would you consider to be an important realization you have had this week from your study of these lessons?

2. How have the Scripture passages from this week shown you that the Bible leads us to the Mass and that the biblical history of salvation comes to its completion in the Eucharist?

3. What are some of the parallels and connections between the annual Jewish Passover and the eucharistic liturgy of Christians? (Lesson 1)

4. What do the ancient covenant rituals performed by Moses teach you about the meaning of the Mass? (Lesson 2)

5. If Christ died "once for all," then what is the connection between Christ's sacrificial offering to the Father in heaven and the sacrifice of the Mass? (Lesson 3)

6. Compare the sin offering of the Day of Atonement and Israel's thanksgiving offering. In what sense do they each prefigure different effects of the sacrifice of Christ? (Lessons 3 and 4)

7. What is added to your understanding when you consider the Mass as the thanksgiving offering of the risen Christ? (Lesson 4)

8. What does the Emmaus account of Luke's gospel teach you about the relationship between word and sacrament in the church's liturgy? (Lesson 5)

9. How does the Mass lead you from word to worship, then from worship to witness? (Lesson 5)

10. In what sense is the Mass the union of heaven and earth? (Lesson 6)

11. How does the book of Revelation symbolically express the reality of Christ's eternal sacrifice offered to the Father? (Lesson 6)

12. After discussing this session, what do you most want to think about at Mass this Sunday?

Remind group members to complete the six lessons from section III during the week ahead.

Offer prayers of thanksgiving aloud to God for the insights and understanding you gained in the lesson this week.

Offer prayers for your own needs and the needs of others. Pray for the grace to act upon any decisions or resolutions you have made during your study.

Conclude together: *Glory be to the Father, and to the Son, and to the Holy Spirit …*

Section III

Introductory Rites of the Mass

The word "liturgy" comes from a Greek word meaning "the work of the people." This means that the liturgy is not something we watch as spectators, but something in which we participate and to which we offer God as his people. Liturgy demands a personal investment of ourselves: an external involvement and an interior dedication of our minds and hearts.

Because the eucharistic liturgy demands our full participation, it requires preparation beforehand and readiness for the sacred actions in which we will engage. The purpose of the Introductory Rites, then, is to bring us into the presence of God and to prepare our minds and hearts for the encounter with God that we will enter through word and sacrament.

The rites preceding the Liturgy of the Word, namely the Entrance, Greeting, Act of Penitence, Kyrie, Gloria, and Collect, have the character of a beginning, introduction, and preparation. Their purpose is to ensure that the faithful who come together establish spiritual union and dispose themselves to listen properly to God's word and to celebrate the Eucharist worthily. These Introductory Rites happen rather quickly, so if we arrive late, we will miss key parts of the liturgy that are designed to properly prepare us to celebrate the holy mysteries.

We come to the sacred liturgy, the summit of the church's life, because we have first been called to faith and to conversion. For the goal of all the church's apostolic activity is that all who are made children of God by faith and baptism should come together as his church to praise God, to take part in Christ's sacrifice and to eat the Lord's Supper. When we come for Eucharist, we come with our whole selves and our whole lives, presenting ourselves before our God and saying, "Here I am. I have come to do your will." We want to come not so much to get something from God, but to give ourselves to God who has already given us everything. There is no other action of the church that equals the effectiveness of the Mass. In this sacred offering, God is perfectly glorified and we are sanctified.

But in order that the eucharistic liturgy may be able to produce its full effects in us, we must come with proper dispositions, with our minds attuned to our voice, so that we may cooperate with God's grace. We want to come into God's presence with ears open to hear God speak to us and hearts open to participate in the saving sacrifice of Christ. Full, conscious, and active participation in the Mass by all the people is the church's paramount desire. We gather to experience the marriage of God and his people, of Christ and his church. As the bride of Christ we cry, "Come, Lord Jesus," and we prepare ourselves in order to be ready for the bridegroom.

We come together for the church's liturgy as a pilgrim people with longing hearts, much like our ancestors in Israel came to the temple to worship God. But in Christ we ourselves become a holy temple of the Lord, a dwelling place for God in the Spirit. We come before God not as strangers or silent spectators, but as brother and sisters of Jesus, sharing a spiritual kinship as the family of God. We are at home, experiencing a sense of belonging as members of Christ's church. We realize that Jesus is present with us as the church begins to pray and sing, for he has promised, "Where two or three are gathered in my name, I am there among them" (Matt 18:20).

- What is the main purpose of the Introductory Rites?

- Why is it necessary that we prepare our minds and hearts for the liturgy?

- How can I experience full and active participation in the Mass?

Processing to the House and Altar of God

LISTENING

Read or chant these psalms that were originally a single song. Join in spirit with the throngs of God's people through the ages who sang these words as an expression of their longing to worship God.

Psalm 42:1–6

¹As a deer longs for flowing streams,
    so my soul longs for you, O God.
²My soul thirsts for God,
    for the living God.
When shall I come and behold
    the face of God?
³My tears have been my food
    day and night,
while people say to me continually,
    "Where is your God?"

⁴These things I remember,
    as I pour out my soul:
how I went with the throng,
    and led them in procession to the house of God,
with glad shouts and songs of thanksgiving,
    a multitude keeping festival.
⁵Why are you cast down, O my soul,
    and why are you disquieted within me?
Hope in God; for I shall again praise him,
    my help ⁶and my God.

Psalm *43:1–5*

¹Vindicate me, O God, and defend my cause
  against an ungodly people;
from those who are deceitful and unjust
  deliver me!
²For you are the God in whom I take refuge;
  why have you cast me off?
Why must I walk about mournfully
  because of the oppression of the enemy?

³O send out your light and your truth;
  let them lead me;
let them bring me to your holy hill
  and to your dwelling.
⁴Then I will go to the altar of God,
  to God my exceeding joy;
and I will praise you with the harp,
  O God, my God.
⁵Why are you cast down, O my soul,
  and why are you disquieted within me?
Hope in God; for I shall again praise him,
  my help and my God.

UNDERSTANDING

Continue learning about the context of these psalms so they can lead you to worship at God's altar.

In preparation for the weekly eucharistic liturgy, disciples of Jesus gather together from their homes and activities of the week into one place on the Lord's day. As members of the church, we greet one another upon arrival, recognizing our spiritual kinship that gives us a sense of belonging and comfort. We prepare our hearts to celebrate the sacred mysteries of Christ's church.

The entrance antiphon or hymn then begins as the priest enters with the deacon and other liturgical ministers. The procession reminds us that we are a people on pilgrimage who travel together on our way to the Father. In the ancient church, often the people walked in procession with the celebrant — a practice we still follow in some forms for major feasts. The purpose of the accompanying chant is to promote the unity of the assembly and introduce the thoughts of the congregation to the liturgical season or feast. The church's liturgy attaches great importance to singing, since Paul the apostle urged the faithful who gather to await the Lord's coming to "sing psalms, hymns, and spiritual songs" (Col 3:16). As St. Augustine said, "Singing is for one who loves."

Many of the psalms were written to accompany the journey of the Israelites up to the temple in Jerusalem. These were sung primarily for the great pilgrimage feasts of Passover, Pentecost, and Tabernacles. These songs are filled with a sense of the joy and privilege of going to the house of the Lord to worship him. Psalms 42 and 43 express a deep desire to come into God's presence, and for that reason, have often been used as a preparation for the eucharistic celebration.

In these psalms there are numerous liturgical references. We find mention of the temple, the throng, the procession, songs of thanksgiving, the festival (42:4), God's dwelling, and God's altar (43:3–4). The poet nostalgically recalls participating in liturgical worship at the temple in the past and longs to do so again. Though exiled from Jerusalem, the singer expresses confident hope that he or she will again come to God's dwelling and offer joyful praise (42:5).

The psalmist expresses the soul's longing for God as an unquenched thirst (42:1–2). Life apart from the face of God is like a deer longing for flowing streams in the wilderness. His captives sarcastically ask, "Where is your God?" As the singer pours out his soul, his wrenching sadness is compounded by the fact that he cannot vent feelings with anyone who understands. In the same way that separation from home and loved ones makes memories more intense and the emptiness more painful, the psalmist feels the absence of God and longs to return to the divine presence. The exile holds on to his hope in God, and asks God to send out his divine light and truth to lead him back to Jerusalem and to God's dwelling (43:3).

The psalmist recalls the pilgrim feasts of Israel and anticipates returning to celebrate the feasts in solemn worship. In anticipation of God's leading him back, the psalmist says, "Then I will go to the altar of God, to God my exceeding joy" (43:4). The mention of the altar recalls that sacrifice is an integral part of worshiping God. Celebrating a feast or giving thanks or renewing a covenant always involves offering sacrifice at the altar.

Since the eucharistic liturgy is the sacrifice of the new covenant, God's people gather around the altar of God. When the liturgical ministers reach the sanctuary, they reverence the altar with a profound bow. As an expression of veneration, the priest and deacon also kiss the altar, and on occasion, the priest may incense the altar as the holy sacrifice of the Mass begins.

REFLECTING

Spend some time seeking to identify your feelings with those of the psalmist. Reflect on these questions in an attempt to deepen your desire for God.

- The psalmist describes his yearning for God as a deep thirst. How would you describe your feelings during a time in which you were away from eucharistic worship? What metaphor might describe your yearning for God's presence?

- The psalmist expresses his memory of processing to the temple for the feasts of Israel. What elements of these psalms indicate that the church's eucharistic worship is rooted in the worship of the Israelites in the temple?

- The bow of the priests and liturgical ministers at the altar and the kiss expresses the reverence that all God's people should have for the altar of God. Why is the altar so central to the church's architecture, and why is it given such honor in the liturgy?

PRAYING

Respond to God's word with heartfelt prayer. As you pray this prayer, let it be an incentive to continue with your own.

- Gracious God, you call your people to take on the heart of a pilgrim on the way to you. Deepen my longing for your presence and increase my yearning to honor you with songs of thanksgiving and sacrificial worship.

When words are no longer necessary or helpful in your prayer, simply rest in God's presence and praise him with your heart.

ACTING

Our own entrance procession and preparation for celebrating the holy mysteries begins on our way to church. As we fast and prepare our hearts to worship, we should consider our journey to Mass as the first phase of our participation.

- What can I do to overcome the inevitable distractions of traffic and worries on the way to church so that I can prepare myself for worship? How can I arrive with sufficient time to greet others and to enter a spirit of prayer before Mass begins?

LESSON 8

Marked with the Sign of the Cross in the Name of the Trinity

█ LISTENING

Realize that you have been chosen and claimed by Jesus the Lord. Listen to how the New Testament writers express the meaning of being alive in Christ.

Matthew 28:19–20

[19]"Go therefore and make disciples of all nations, baptizing them in the name of the Father and of the Son and of the Holy Spirit, [20]and teaching them to obey everything that I have commanded you. And remember, I am with you always, to the end of the age."

Romans 6:3–11

[3]Do you not know that all of us who have been baptized into Christ Jesus were baptized into his death? [4]Therefore we have been buried with him by baptism into death, so that, just as Christ was raised from the dead by the glory of the Father, so we too might walk in newness of life.

[5]For if we have been united with him in a death like his, we will certainly be united with him in a resurrection like his. [6]We know that our old self was crucified with him so that the body of sin might be destroyed, and we might no longer be enslaved to sin. [7]For whoever has died is freed from sin. [8]But if we have died with Christ, we believe that we will also live with him. [9]We know that Christ, being raised from the dead, will never die again; death no longer has dominion over him. [10]The death he died, he died to sin, once for all; but the life he lives, he lives to God. [11]So you also must consider yourselves dead to sin and alive to God in Christ Jesus.

Revelation 14:1–3

¹Then I looked, and there was the Lamb, standing on Mount Zion! And with him were one hundred forty-four thousand who had his name and his Father's name written on their foreheads. ²And I heard a voice from heaven like the sound of many waters and like the sound of loud thunder; the voice I heard was like the sound of harpists playing on their harps, ³and they sing a new song before the throne and before the four living creatures and before the elders. No one could learn that song except the one hundred forty-four thousand who have been redeemed from the earth.

UNDERSTANDING

After allowing these inspired texts to penetrate your mind and heart, let them help you understand what it means to be sealed with the sign of the cross.

In the opening gesture of the Mass, the priest and people mark themselves with the sign of the cross. The priest says, "In the name of the Father, and of the Son, and of the Holy Spirit," and the faithful give their solemn assent as they answer, "Amen." The words are derived from Jesus' command in the Great Commission that the church should baptize new disciples "in the name of the Father and of the Son and of the Holy Spirit" (Matt 28:19). When we pray in the name of the Trinity, we not only express our belief and commitment to God as Father, Son, and Holy Spirit, but we draw near to God and engage God's power. For when God made his covenant with Israel, he promised, "In every place where I cause my name to be remembered I will come to you and bless you" (Exod 20:24). When we pray in the name of the Father, Son, and Holy Spirit, we become aware that God is powerfully present with us and that we are blessed by God's work of creation, salvation, and sanctification.

The sign of the cross is an ancient gesture that briefly sums up the truth of the Christian life. Beginning with the Israelite ritual of marking the forehead with an X (*taw* in Hebrew) as a sign of commitment to God and protection from danger (Ezek 9:4), the gesture took on a specifically Christian form in the church's early baptismal rituals. The baptized were marked with the sign of the cross on their foreheads as they were claimed for Christ. The book of Revelation expresses the meaning of this Christian mark of identity as the visionary sees the redeemed multitude bearing the name of Christ the Lamb and his Father's name "written on their foreheads" (Rev 14:1). With this "seal" of God on their foreheads, they are spared from destruction and called to participate in the heavenly liturgy (Rev 7:3; 22:4). Paul says that God anoints us "by putting his seal on us" (2 Cor 1:22) and that the Christian is "marked with the seal" of the Holy Spirit (Eph 1:13; 4:30).

In the ancient world, soldiers and slaves, as well as animals, were "sealed" with the insignia of their owner. With this physical marking, often either a brand or a tattoo, the owner laid claim on them and protected them from danger or theft. At baptism and confirmation, Christians are anointed with the oil of chrism as the ordained minister marks the sign of the cross on their forehead. Imprinted with the sign and seal of the holy Trinity, the believer is claimed as God's own and authenticated as a baptized disciple of Jesus Christ. St. Cyril of Jerusalem, addressing candidates for Christian initiation in the fourth century, invited them to "come, receive the sacramental seal so that you may be easily recognized by the Master."

In time the sign of the cross was multiplied to mark other parts of the body. At the Rite of Acceptance into the catechumenate of the early centuries, the candidates preparing for baptism were marked by their sponsors with the sign of the cross over their forehead, ears, eyes, lips, heart, shoulders, hands, and feet. The sign of the cross eventually became a striking gesture that marked the whole body of a baptized Christian.

The sign of the cross should always be connected in our minds with Christian baptism. It not only reminds us of our baptism, but it releases the sacrament's power in our lives. The external sign expresses an interior grace, the very life of the triune God within us. Paul explains that, in the baptismal water, our old self was crucified with Christ and buried with him, so that we might rise from the water and walk in newness of life (Romans 6:4–6). The font of baptism is both a tomb and a womb. St. Cyril of Jerusalem elaborated on this theme in his mystagogical sermons to new Christians:

> Then you were led to the holy pool of divine baptism, as Christ was carried from the cross to the tomb.... And each of you was asked whether he believed in the name of the Father, and of the Son, and of the Holy Spirit. You made that saving confession and you descended three times into the water and ascended, symbolizing the three days of Christ's burial.... For by this immersion and rising you were both dying and being born. That water of salvation was at once your grave and your mother.

By baptism we are immersed and entrusted into the name of the Trinitarian God, so in making the sign of the cross we repeat the baptismal formula and renew our faith in God the Father, Son, and Holy Spirit. In baptism we are buried and rise with Christ, so in making the sign of the cross we consider ourselves "dead to sin and alive to God in Christ Jesus" (Rom 6:11). In baptism we are sealed in the Holy Spirit, so in making the sign of the cross we proclaim that we belong to Christ and are his disciples. And as newborn sons and daughters of the Father, we have gained access to the family table of the Lord's Supper. This baptismal meaning of the sign of the cross is brought out even more clearly when we sign ourselves with baptismal water as we enter the church, and when the blessing and sprinkling of water replaces the penitential act, especially during the Sundays of the Easter season. The water used in these rituals may be either water from the church's baptismal font or water specifically blessed as a reminder of baptism. Making the sign of the cross with this water, then, explicitly connects the sign of the cross with baptismal water and expresses our desire to continually walk in the new life we received at baptism.

REFLECTING

Consider the sign of the cross as a simple yet richly meaningful gesture that sums up the truth of the Christian life.

- Just as the mark of circumcision expressed one's participation in the old covenant, the mark of baptism — the sign of the cross — expresses each one's participation in the new covenant. Why is the sign of the cross so ideal as the opening gesture of the Mass?

  unity of all sealed in Holy Spirit, all striving to be with God

- The baptismal seal on our forehead reminds us that we belong to Christ, that we can call on his help and protection, and that we are called to share in his Supper. What meaning of the sign of the cross is most new to me? Which meaning would I like to focus on next Sunday?

  That it expresses the life of God within me. It marks me as belonging to him.

- Paul says that we are baptized into the dying and rising of Christ. Cyril of Jerusalem says that the waters of salvation are both your grave and your mother. What are the implications of this truth for my Christian life? What does it mean for me to "walk in newness of life"?

PRAYING

Make the sign of the cross. Trace the vertical bar, from your forehead to your breast, to pledge your love and devotion to God. Trace the horizontal bar, from shoulder to shoulder, to pledge your love and service to others.

- Lord God, you call me to love you with all my heart, mind, and strength, and to love my neighbor as myself. Since I have been immersed in the baptismal waters of new life, give me strength to do your will and the courage to give my life as a disciple of your Son, Jesus.

Make the sign of the cross again slowly, asking God to empower your life with the grace of your baptism and to give you a deep hunger for the family table of his Eucharist.

ACTING

Consider the ways that making the sign of the cross can influence your daily life.

- By tracing the sign of the cross upon my body, I declare that as a disciple of Jesus, I no longer belong to myself, but I belong to him. My body, my time, my heart, my life belongs to Christ. How can my daily choices and my lifestyle better express the reality that Christ owns my life?

The Grace of our Lord Jesus Christ Be with Your Spirit

LISTENING

Read aloud the words of these texts from Paul's letters so that you not only read them with your eyes but hear them proclaimed with your ears. Note any words or phrases that strike you personally as you consider the new life you have been given in Christ.

Romans 1:1–7

¹Paul, a servant of Jesus Christ, called to be an apostle, set apart for the gospel of God, ²which he promised beforehand through his prophets in the holy scriptures, ³the gospel concerning his Son, who was descended from David according to the flesh ⁴and was declared to be Son of God with power according to the spirit of holiness by resurrection from the dead, Jesus Christ our Lord, ⁵through whom we have received grace and apostleship to bring about the obedience of faith among all the Gentiles for the sake of his name, ⁶including yourselves who are called to belong to Jesus Christ,

⁷To all God's beloved in Rome, who are called to be saints:

Grace to you and peace from God our Father and the Lord Jesus Christ.

Sometimes mass intro.

2 Corinthians 13:11–13

¹¹Finally, brothers and sisters, farewell. Put things in order, listen to my appeal, agree with one another, live in peace; and the God of love and peace will be with you. ¹²Greet one another with a holy kiss. All the saints greet you.

¹³The grace of the Lord Jesus Christ, the love of God, and the communion of the Holy Spirit be with all of you.

Philippians 4:21–23

²¹Greet every saint in Christ Jesus. The friends who are with me greet you. ²²All the saints greet you, especially those of the emperor's household.

²³The grace of the Lord Jesus Christ be with your spirit.

UNDERSTANDING

Try to discern the deeper significance and meaning of these Pauline texts through the commentary that follows.

Following the sign of the cross, the priest welcomes the congregation with an apostolic greeting. The three options for this greeting are taken from common salutations from the biblical literature and especially from the letters of Paul. The welcome is formalized and taken from scriptural language because the priest greets the people in his sacramental role and is addressing the assembly called together by God.

The salutation from Paul's letters, "Grace to you and peace from God our Father and the Lord Jesus Christ" (Rom 1:7), is one of the greetings that may introduce the liturgy. All thirteen of the Pauline letters contain this characteristic greeting in their introductory verses. It is a remarkable combination of a Greek salutation, grace (*charis*), which seems to summarize the gospel in a single word, and the ancient Hebrew blessing, peace (*shalom*), which expresses the fullness of well-being that God desires for his people. In this uniquely Christian greeting, Paul addresses Gentile and Jewish believers together, as members of the one church.

Notice that Paul did not write, "Charis to you Greeks and shalom to you Hebrews." Grace is not just for Gentiles and peace is not just for Jews. God desires the whole body of Christ to receive God's grace and to experience his shalom. Writing to congregations that were often divided and torn by factional strife, Paul's greeting was a concrete reminder to each church that they were called to be a countercultural reality, a "new creation." The church is not a congregation created by simply linking Jews and Gentiles together, but a united body of Christ, a transformed people made new in the Risen Lord.

When this greeting is used to welcome people to the eucharistic liturgy, it demonstrates that the church is unlike any other social order. It joins together vastly dissimilar people into a higher unity — oneness in Christ. In Paul's day, the world was divided between Jews and Gentiles, slave and free, women and men, rich and poor. But Paul dared to imagine a Christian community that not only included all of these, but also brought them into interdependent relationships. At least part of the dramatic witness of the church in the first century was this attractive, alternative new society that it offered to the world.

Today our culture continues to be divided between race, class, gender, politics, and many other divisions, and we find these variations within the church as well. Yet, when we listen to Paul and follow the way of Jesus, we realize that our common identity transcends our differences. Through this greeting at the beginning of the Mass, the church urges us to treat one another with love — to extend grace and to make peace with one another. In that way, we break down boundaries, we become truly Catholic, and we become a powerful witness of Christ to our world.

Another option for the liturgy's opening greeting comes from the end of Paul's second letter to the Corinthians: "The grace of our Lord Jesus Christ, and the love of God, and the communion of the Holy Spirit be with you all" (2 Cor 13:13). Paul wishes for the community three key aspects of the Christian life. From Christ comes the grace by which people receive redemption from sin and death. Behind this grace stands the love of God from which salvation begins and continues to flow through the community. The communion given by the Holy Spirit is the fellowship in which all the believers are called to live. Paul prays that grace, love, and communion be given by the trinitarian God to the whole congregation Paul addresses. When this apostolic greeting is used at the beginning of the liturgy, the church prays that these same gifts of the Christian life be given for the sake of the unity and salvation of the congregation addressed.

The final optional greeting, "The Lord be with you," is a common greeting throughout the Bible (Ruth 2:4; Judg 6:12; 2 Chron 15:2), including the salutation used by the angel Gabriel to greet Mary (Luke 1:28). There is no verb in the Greek text, so it may be translated in the indicative, "The Lord is with you," or the subjunctive, "The Lord be with you." In the Great Commission of Matthew's gospel, Jesus promises to be with his people to the end, "I am with you always" (Matt 28:20). So this liturgical greeting, "The Lord be with you," connects us with God's faithful people throughout the ages and with our confident assurance of the presence of Jesus.

The people's response to all three of these options, "And with your spirit," is also derived from Paul's writings. At the end of his letter to the Philippians, Paul concludes with a blessing for the whole community: "The grace of the Lord Jesus Christ be with your spirit" (Phil 4:23; see also Gal 6:18; Philemon 1:25). He also concludes the second letter to Timothy by addressing his friend in these words: "The Lord be with your spirit" (2 Tim 4:22). Paul wants his Christian friends to be freed from a spirit of selfishness or dejection and to take on the spirit of Christ that brings hope and purpose to life. In the church's liturgy there is a long tradition, going back at least to the early third century, of dividing this blessing into two phrases: *"Dominus vobiscum"* (The Lord be with you) and the response, *"Et cum spiritu tuo"* (And with your spirit).

The two parts express a mutual desire that the Lord will be present among the people and with God's ordained minister.

"With your spirit" is a more expressive and intensive way of saying "with you." The spirit is one's innermost self, the inner outlook and will that governs one's thoughts and actions. To pray that the Lord be with your spirit asks that the Lord be your light, your joy, your companion, the source of your words and deeds. The return to the more traditional and literal response, "And with your spirit," rather than the more colloquial "And also with you," accomplishes several things. It associates the response more closely with the language of Paul, it aligns the language with the ancient liturgical tradition of the church, and it affirms the spiritual nature of the community assembled for worship. This community gathered in the Lord is composed of the priest, who is uniquely blessed with the spiritual gift of ordination, and the people, who are filled with spiritual gifts that make them a consecrated people dedicated to their mission in the world.

REFLECTING

After studying these biblical greetings and blessings, spend some time reflecting on the words we hear and speak in the eucharistic liturgy, allowing these words to penetrate your heart more deeply.

- Paul combines a Greek and a Hebrew blessing in his new Christian greeting: "Grace and peace to you." In what way is Paul's salutation uniquely Christian? What does it say about the church?

- Paul ends many of his letters with some form of the prayer, "The Lord be with your spirit." How does Paul's wish for his communities express both the final promise of Jesus in Matthew's gospel (Matt 28:20) and the final hope expressed in the book of Revelation (Rev 22:20–21).

(Matt.) "...teaching them to observe all that I have commanded you; + lo, I am with you always, to the close of the age."
(Rev.) He who testifies to these things says, Surely I am coming soon." Amen. Come, Lord Jesus! The grace of the Lord Jesus be with all the saints, Amen.

- In all the major languages of the world, the Latin "*Et cum spiritu tuo*" is translated literally by including a form of the word "*spiritus.*" Why is the people's liturgical response, "And with your spirit," a richer and more biblical response than the less formal "And also with you"?

PRAYING

Spend a few moments in silence, praying, "Come, Lord Jesus," and asking that the Lord make his presence known to you.

- Lord Jesus, open my heart to your presence and give me the assurance that you are with me always as you promised. Bestow upon me your grace and your peace, and bring the people of your church together with the gifts of unity.

Continue praying, asking God to rid you of a selfish or dejected spirit and enliven within you a spirit of wisdom, joy, and generosity.

ACTING

Prepare for your Sunday worship by reviewing the greetings and responses of the liturgy.

- Note how many times we participate in the dialogue, "The Lord be with you… And with your spirit." In which parts of the Mass are they found? How can I participate more consciously in these liturgical exchanges?

LESSON 10

Lord, Have Mercy, for I Have Sinned

LISTENING

Read or chant this psalm and gospel text, calling on God's merciful forgiveness. Trust that God forgives when we confess our sins to him and that Christ has mercy on those who call out to him.

Psalm 51:1–12

[1]Have mercy on me, O God,
   according to your steadfast love;
according to your abundant mercy
   blot out my transgressions.
[2]Wash me thoroughly from my iniquity,
   and cleanse me from my sin.

[3]For I know my transgressions,
   and my sin is ever before me.
[4]Against you, you alone, have I sinned,
   and done what is evil in your sight,
so that you are justified in your sentence
   and blameless when you pass judgment.
[5]Indeed, I was born guilty,
   a sinner when my mother conceived me.

[6]You desire truth in the inward being;
   therefore teach me wisdom in my secret heart.
[7]Purge me with hyssop, and I shall be clean;
   wash me, and I shall be whiter than snow.
[8]Let me hear joy and gladness;
   let the bones that you have crushed rejoice.

[9]Hide your face from my sins,
   and blot out all my iniquities.

[10]Create in me a clean heart, O God,
   and put a new and right spirit within me.
[11]Do not cast me away from your presence,
   and do not take your holy spirit from me.
[12]Restore to me the joy of your salvation,
   and sustain in me a willing spirit.

Matthew 20:29–34

[29]As they were leaving Jericho, a large crowd followed him. [30]There were two blind men sitting by the roadside. When they heard that Jesus was passing by, they shouted, "Lord, have mercy on us, Son of David!" [31]The crowd sternly ordered them to be quiet; but they shouted even more loudly, "Have mercy on us, Lord, Son of David!" [32]Jesus stood still and called them, saying, "What do you want me to do for you?" [33]They said to him, "Lord, let our eyes be opened." [34]Moved with compassion, Jesus touched their eyes. Immediately they regained their sight and followed him.

UNDERSTANDING

After a careful reading, continue listening for the ways the psalmist and the blind man call out for God's mercy and bring you to a spirit of penance.

Throughout the Scriptures, those who encounter the living God become painfully aware of their own sinfulness and unworthiness to come into his presence. The greatest penitent in Scripture is King David, who said to God, "I have sinned greatly in that I have done this thing. But now, I pray you, take away the guilt of your servant" (1 Chron 21:8). In the tradition of Israel, Psalm 51, the great penitential prayer of the Bible, has been ascribed to David. This magnificent prayer from a repentant heart has been prayed in the temple of Israel and in churches through the ages. Through Psalm 51, the Miserere, the sinner humbly acknowledges that he has sinned and asks for God's merciful forgiveness. The penitent implores God, "Have mercy on me," "wash me," "cleanse me," "blot out my iniquities." He pleads, "Create in me a clean heart," and, "Restore to me the joy of your salvation."

Introducing the Penitential Act of the Mass, the celebrant says, "Let us acknowledge our sins, that we may prepare ourselves to celebrate the sacred mysteries." As the Israelite may have prayed Psalm 51 as preparation for prayer in the temple or offering sacrifice, the Christian prays the Confiteor before encountering the presence of God in word and sacrament. Our listening to the humble prayer of David can help us pray the Penitential Act with heartfelt meaning. Like the psalm, the Confiteor expresses the alienation that sin causes by addressing God in the singular "I." Each individual responds, "I confess…" It is one of the few places in the liturgy where a worshiper speaks as an "I" rather than as part of a "we." The individual confesses his or her own offenses, personal responsibility for the sins of communities, and complicity in the sinful structures in the world.

Each of us, like David, confess "that I have greatly sinned," in thought, word, and deed. The triple repetition, "through my fault, through my fault, through my most grievous fault," while striking the breast, is a way of emphasizing the dreadfulness of sin and of taking personal responsibility for it. The gesture of striking the breast was a Jewish sign of deep sorrow for one's sinfulness. In Jesus' parable, he says, "The tax collector, standing far off, would not even look up to heaven, but was beating his breast and saying, 'God, be merciful to me, a sinner!'" (Luke 18:13). St. Augustine, in the early fifth century, noted,

> No sooner have you heard the word "Confiteor" than you strike your breast. What does this mean except that you wish to bring to light what is concealed in the breast, and by this act to cleanse your hidden sins? (*Sermo de verbis Domini*, 13).

Our bodily actions, when done with consciousness and understanding, can affect our interior disposition and help make spiritual truths real for us. When I admit my fault and strike my breast with a contrite spirit, God will indeed "create in me a clean heart" (Ps 51:10).

Following the Confiteor, or when another option is used for the Penitential Act, the congregation sings or speaks the Kyrie Eleison, either in its original Greek or translated as "Lord have mercy." The cry for God's mercy runs throughout the Scriptures and mercy is one of God's greatest attributes. Like David, who pleads, "Have mercy on me, O God" (Ps 51:1), we beseech God with humility and hope, for something that we cannot do for ourselves.

At the beginning of the eucharistic liturgy, we are like the blind beggars of the gospel when they heard that Jesus was passing by (Matt 20:30). They cannot see him, so they persistently beg, "Lord, have mercy." They cried out to Jesus until he heard them and healed them, then they followed Jesus to his passion and triumph in Jerusalem. We desperately need the mercy of Christ because we miss seeing him because of our sin. When he heals us and opens our eyes, we are able to participate in his sacrifice and share in his eternal life.

REFLECTING

As you spend some time reflecting on the liturgical act of penitence, try to personalize God's healing and forgiveness as you experience a sense of your own sinfulness.

- Under the old covenant, priests and people often cleansed themselves in some way, through fasting or ritual washing, before entering the temple or offering sacrifice. What are some of the ways the Penitential Act of the Mass helps us prepare to experience Christ?

- The physical gesture of striking the breast during our admission of fault in the Confiteor helps us express our interior repentance. Why are words and physical signs important for expressing inner dispositions? What are some other bodily gestures that express an interior reality during the Mass?

- Hebrew, Greek, and Latin are the three languages in which was written the inscription identifying Jesus on the cross (John 19:20). The liturgy contains acclamations in all three languages: Hebrew (Alleluia, Hosanna, and Amen), Greek (Kyrie eleison), and Latin (Sanctus and Agnus Dei). Why is it important that Catholic Christians learn a few phrases in these three languages?

PRAYING

After reflecting on the prayers of Scripture with a desire to take them to heart, pray again Psalm 51 with understanding and sincerity.

- Turn again to Psalm 51 and pray this ancient prayer from the heart. Ask God to have mercy on you, to grant you forgiveness, to create a clean heart within you, and to restore the joy of your salvation.

Continue contemplating the presence of Christ, asking him to open your eyes.

ACTING

The sacrament of the Eucharist frees us from venial sin and preserves us from deadly sin. However, the Eucharist is not ordered to the forgiveness of mortal sin, which is proper to the sacrament of reconciliation.

- Consider receiving the sacrament of penance either communally or privately this week, so that you may receive absolution from sin and be fully reconciled with God and his church.

Singing "Glory to God in the Highest" and "Peace on Earth"

▋LISTENING

Listen to these inspired voices as they tell of the angels and saints giving glory to God in heaven and on earth. Join in their joyous praise of God the heavenly King and of the Lamb of God, Son of the Father.

Luke 2:8–14

[8]In that region there were shepherds living in the fields, keeping watch over their flock by night. [9]Then an angel of the Lord stood before them, and the glory of the Lord shone around them, and they were terrified. [10]But the angel said to them, "Do not be afraid; for see — I am bringing you good news of great joy for all the people: [11]to you is born this day in the city of David a Savior, who is the Messiah, the Lord. [12]This will be a sign for you: you will find a child wrapped in bands of cloth and lying in a manger." [13]And suddenly there was with the angel a multitude of the heavenly host, praising God and saying,

> [14]"Glory to God in the highest heaven,
> and on earth peace among those whom he favors!"

Revelation 7:9–17

[9]After this I looked, and there was a great multitude that no one could count, from every nation, from all tribes and peoples and languages, standing before the throne and before the Lamb, robed in white, with palm branches in their hands. [10]They cried out in a loud voice, saying,

> "Salvation belongs to our God who is seated on the throne,
> and to the Lamb!" [11]

And all the angels stood around the throne and around the elders and the four living creatures, and they fell on their faces before the throne and worshiped God, [12]singing,

> "Amen! Blessing and glory and wisdom
> and thanksgiving and honor
> and power and might
> be to our God forever and ever! Amen."

[13]Then one of the elders addressed me, saying, "Who are these, robed in white, and where have they come from?" [14]I said to him, "Sir, you are the one that knows." Then he said to me, "These are they who have come out of the great ordeal; they have washed their robes and made them white in the blood of the Lamb.

> [15]For this reason they are before the throne of God,
> > and worship him day and night within his temple,
> > and the one who is seated on the throne will shelter them.
> [16]They will hunger no more, and thirst no more;
> > the sun will not strike them,
> > nor any scorching heat;
> [17]for the Lamb at the center of the throne will be their shepherd,
> > and he will guide them to springs of the water of life,
> and God will wipe away every tear from their eyes."

UNDERSTANDING

Continue searching to understand the song of the angels and realizing the presence of the angels with you when you worship God in the Mass.

The Gloria is a beautiful hymn of praise, sometimes called the *hymnus angelicus*. Its opening declaration is formed from the words of the angelic choir that first greeted the birth of Jesus in Bethlehem (Luke 2:14). The entire hymn is woven from biblical phrases and composed to resemble the psalms and canticles of Scripture. It is one of the earliest post-biblical examples of hymnody in the ancient church.

The hymn was composed first in Greek, in either the second or third century. Its beauty is a witness to the splendor of lyric poetry produced by Christians during the age of persecution. The hymn became part of the festal matins (morning prayer) of the Eastern rites, then was translated into Latin and gradually entered the Mass of the Roman rite.

The Gloria is sung or recited on Sundays outside the seasons of Advent and Lent, and on solemnities and feasts. This hymn of praise has been set to a wide variety of melodies through the centuries, from plainchant to recent compositions. Among its most famous musical settings are those by Palestrina, Bach, Mozart, and Beethoven. In the Mass of today, it may be intoned by the priest, a cantor, or the choir. It may be sung either by the congregation together, or by the people alternately with the choir, or by the choir alone.

The birth of the incarnate Christ in Bethlehem brought together the two worlds of heaven and earth. The angelic anthem consists of two parts: proclaiming "glory to God in the highest heaven" and evoking "peace on earth" among the people so privileged to receive the birth of the Savior. Though there is a sharp contrast between God's heavenly glory and our earthly reality, the Scriptures help us believe that these two worlds are in open communication. The birth of a child in Bethlehem can evoke the choirs of heaven, and the angels can descend on lowly shepherds and sing of God's glory.

This same unity of heaven and earth occurs at the eucharistic liturgy. We join with the angels in heavenly worship and they join with us in our earthly liturgy. St. John Chrysostom in the fourth century said, "When Mass is celebrated the sanctuary is filled with countless angels who adore the divine victim immolated on the altar." Pope Gregory the Great in the sixth century said, "The heavens open and multitudes of angels come to assist in the holy sacrifice of the Mass." The book of Revelation offers us a vision of heavenly worship of God and the Lamb by a great multitude of redeemed humanity (Rev 7:9). All the angels stand around the throne worshiping God and singing a hymn of praise to the glory of God (Rev 7:11–12). Though our ultimate destiny is to give glory to God with the angels of heaven, we are joined with them now in each celebration of the Mass. As we sing the Gloria in the liturgy, we not only recall the praise of angels to the incarnate Christ in Bethlehem, but anticipate the praise we will give to the glorified Christ forever. How right it is to sing those words of the angels as we prepare to receive the living Christ under the sacramental signs of our Eucharist.

REFLECTING

Reflect on the words and phrases of the Gloria in light of the Scriptures from Luke and Revelations, then use your new understanding to sing greater praise to God.

- The book of Revelation was written during the first century persecution of the church by the Roman Empire, and those who sing the hymn to God's glory are "they who have come out of the great ordeal" (Rev 7:14). The Gloria was written by the early Christians during a later period of persecution in the second or third century. How do periods of trial and suffering draw out such magnificent poetry and music in praise of God?

- In poetry and music it is not unusual to use a variety of different words to express the same idea. The angels offer to God a sevenfold attribution of praise (Rev 7:12). In the Gloria, five verbs are used to refer to our actions in response to God's graciousness: "We praise you, we bless you, we adore you, we glorify you, we give you thanks for your great glory." What do these multiplications of words express about the human and angelic praise of God?

- List the numerous biblical titles of Jesus that are proclaimed in the Gloria. Each of these titles expresses a different aspect of his role in our salvation. On which of these titles would I like to meditate in prayer?

  Lord God   *Holy One*
  heavenly King   *Most High*
  Almighty Father
  Lamb of God
  Only begotten Son

PRAYING

Pray with the words of the angels and the words that spring from your own relationship with God.

- Lord God, heavenly King and almighty Father, We praise you, we bless you, we adore you, we glorify you, we give you thanks for your great glory. May we praise your name on earth as it is in heaven.

Continue praising God in words that come from your own heart.

ACTING

Consider the opportunities during the day when you could offer a word or gesture of praise to God.

- How can I make praise of God a more regular part of my Christian life? What could change if I offered praise to God during several moments throughout my day?

Praying to the Father, through Jesus Christ, in the Holy Spirit

■ LISTENING

Breathe in, being filled with the presence of God's Spirit. Breathe out, letting go of all that could distract you from this sacred time. Trust that the Holy Spirit who inspired these texts is alive within you so that you can hear God's word.

Romans 8:14–17, 26–27

[14]For all who are led by the Spirit of God are children of God. [15]For you did not receive a spirit of slavery to fall back into fear, but you have received a spirit of adoption. When we cry, "Abba! Father!" [16]it is that very Spirit bearing witness with our spirit that we are children of God, [17]and if children, then heirs, heirs of God and joint heirs with Christ — if, in fact, we suffer with him so that we may also be glorified with him.

[26]Likewise the Spirit helps us in our weakness; for we do not know how to pray as we ought, but that very Spirit intercedes with sighs too deep for words. [27]And God, who searches the heart, knows what is the mind of the Spirit, because the Spirit intercedes for the saints according to the will of God.

2 Corinthians 1:19–22

[19]For the Son of God, Jesus Christ, whom we proclaimed among you, Silvanus and Timothy and I, was not "Yes and No"; but in him it is always "Yes." [20]For in him every one of God's promises is a "Yes." For this reason it is through him that we say the "Amen," to the glory of God. [21]But it is God who establishes us with you in Christ and has anointed us, [22]by putting his seal on us and giving us his Spirit in our hearts as a first installment.

UNDERSTANDING

Study these texts so that the words and example of Paul will help you pray better throughout your celebration of the Mass.

The Introductory Rites of the liturgy conclude with a brief, focused prayer called the "Collect," pronounced with the stress on the first syllable. All the other introductory rituals have brought us from a sinful world into the presence of God, preparing us to hear God's word. These preparatory movements find their culmination in the Collect. The text is chanted or spoken by the celebrant and serves to summarize or collect our individual prayers as well as to state a theme of the particular liturgy being celebrated.

First, the celebrant offers the invitation, "Let us pray," followed by a moment of silence. The summons to pray does not refer just to the collect itself. The silent pause invites each member of the congregation to offer private prayer, either a brief prayer that looks forward to what we are about to celebrate or a silent moment contemplating the presence of God. So when the priest says, "Let us pray," that is indeed what we should do.

When we are summoned to pray at this moment, we may still be distracted and unable to focus. We can transform the priest's invitation into our petition to God: "Let us pray, allow us to pray, permit us to pray, enable us to pray, make it possible for us to pray." Paul speaks of this inability to pray and assures us that God's Spirit prays within us: "The Spirit helps us in our weakness; for we do not know how to pray as we ought, but that very Spirit intercedes with sighs too deep for words." (Rom 8:26). We may ask in this quiet moment for the grace of the Spirit so that we are not just bodily present at Mass, but present in mind and heart. We may ask for the grace to pray as we ought, because in our weakness we do not know how. We will then be confident that the Spirit is praying within us, and we will know that it is a prayer that God hears within our hearts (Rom 8:27).

The celebrant then concludes this moment of silent prayer with the Collect, a prayer whose purpose is to collect all the individual prayers into one brief, summary prayer. In the earliest period of the church, the formulation of these prayers was left to the celebrant, who freely extemporized them following a general format. Beginning in the fourth century, many of these Collects were composed in Latin, placed in Sacramentaries, and became increasingly binding upon the celebrant. Many of these ancient prayers are still in use and are characterized by the Roman preference for conciseness and clarity. Traditionally, a collect consisted of a single sentence, often with several clauses, forming a unified petition in a flowing, chanted style.

Through the Collect, the community appears before God and, through the voice of the priest, humbly directs its petitions toward God. The prayer reflects the fact that Christian worship is always trinitarian. It is offered to God through Jesus Christ and in the power of the Holy Spirit. Our prayer, as individuals and as the church, has value only to the extent that it is united to Christ's own prayer and self-offering to his heavenly Father.

The people respond to the prayer offered by the priest with their own "Amen." This is the first of many amens in the liturgy by which the congregation offers its agreement, consent, and commitment. Amen is from a Hebrew root implying truth and steadfastness, and may be translated as "Truly," "So be it," or better yet, "Yes indeed." The response is linked to our collective commitment to God as his people, expressed at several places in the eucharistic liturgy.

We can say "Amen" to the prayers of the liturgy because we know that God is trustworthy. God has spoken a firm and definitive "Amen" to us in Christ. As Paul says, "For in him every one of God's promises is a 'Yes'" (2 Cor 1:20). With Jesus Christ, the answer is always "Yes" to the promises of God. God's "Amen" to us in Christ, then, makes possible and necessary our own "Amen" to God. "It is through him," Paul assures us, "that we say the 'Amen' to the glory of God."

REFLECTING

Think about the way you pray, individually and with the church in liturgy. Consider what you might learn from Paul's teachings and how you might learn to pray better during the church's Eucharist.

- Paul's letter to the Romans helps us understand the movements of the persons of the Trinity as we offer prayer to the Father, through Jesus Christ, and in the power of the Holy Spirit. Why is our prayer effective only through Christ? How does the Holy Spirit help us to pray?

- Through the voice of the priest, our prayer is directed to God and becomes the prayer of the church. What are some ways in which I could be more attuned to the prayer of the church and pray more consciously as a member of God's people in Christ?

- What am I actually saying when I pray "Amen" in response to the prayers of the Mass? How can Paul's teaching in 2 Corinthians help me to voice a more confident and forceful "Amen"?

PRAYING

The Collect teaches us how to pray and makes the prayer of the church our own prayer. Pray this Collect, noticing how it forms a unified petition with a flowing style.

- Almighty God, to whom all hearts are open, all desires known and from whom no secrets are hid; cleanse the thoughts of our hearts by the inspiration of your Holy Spirit, that we may perfectly love you and worthily magnify your holy name, through Jesus Christ our Lord. Amen.

Continue to rest in God's presence, allowing the Holy Spirit to intercede and pray within you.

ACTING

Think back over the elements of the Introductory Rites and what you have realized about them.

- How can I more effectively allow the Introductory Rites to lead me into the presence of God this Sunday? What part of the Introductory Rites can I bring with me into the week in order to live more fully in Christ?

Group Session Guide for Section III

Begin with hospitality and welcome. Offer any announcements or instructions before entering the spirit of focused discussion. Discuss these questions or those of your own choosing:

1. What does full participation in the Mass mean to you? In what sense does the liturgy demand our internal and external involvement?

2. How can you better prepare for worshiping God in the Mass? What is the function of the Introductory Rites?

3. How can you increase your desire for God's presence in the Mass? How do Israel's pilgrimage psalms help you deepen your longing to worship God? (Lesson 7)

4. Why is the altar so central to the church's architecture and why is it given such honor in the liturgy? (Lesson 7)

5. Of all the rich meanings in making the sign of the cross, which has particularly stayed with you this week? (Lesson 8)

6. Which of the apostolic greetings of the Mass do you prefer? What new realization have you gained about that greeting? (Lesson 9)

7. How many times in the Mass do we participate in the dialogue, "The Lord be with you.... And with your spirit"? What does each part of this dialogue mean to you? (Lesson 9)

8. Why did the Israelites acknowledge their sins and ask pardon before offering sacrifice to God? What is the significance of striking the breast while reciting the Confiteor? (Lesson 10)

9. What liturgical words do you know in Hebrew, Greek, and Latin? Are you in favor of retaining the acclamations in their original languages or chanting them in translation? (Lesson 10)

10. What is your favorite phrase of the Gloria? What have you learned about this song that you didn't realize before? (Lesson 11)

11. What are we supposed to do when the priest says, "Let us pray"? What is a Collect and what is its purpose? (Lesson 12)

12. After discussing this session, what can you do to allow the Introductory Rites to more effectively lead you into the presence of God this Sunday?

Remind group members to complete the six lessons from section IV during the week ahead.

Offer prayers of thanksgiving aloud to God for the insights and understanding you gained in the lesson this week.

Offer prayers for your own needs and the needs of others. Pray for the grace to act upon any decisions or resolutions you have made during your study.

Conclude together: *Our Father, who art in heaven …*

Section IV

The Liturgy of the Word

The main part of the Liturgy of the Word is made up of the readings from sacred Scripture together with the chants occurring between them. The first reading is followed by a responsorial psalm, serving as a meditative response to the first reading. The high point of the Liturgy of the Word is the proclamation of the Gospel, which is preceded by the chanting of the Alleluia or another acclamation. The homily develops the biblical readings for the congregation, they affirm their adherence to God's word in the Profession of Faith, and they pour out their petitions in the Prayer of the Faithful for the needs of the entire church and for the salvation of the whole world.

The Liturgy of the Word has its origins in Jewish liturgy as practiced by Jesus and the first Christians. Jesus attended the synagogue and participated in the temple rituals. The church, as described in the Acts of the Apostles, continued to meet in the temple before they shared in the breaking of the bread in their homes. The synagogue service has always been a heavily verbal liturgy, including prayers, psalms, and biblical readings. It also included various Jewish creeds, such as the Shema (Deut 6:4–9), and a range of blessings.

The Hebrew lectionary of Judaism establishes a liturgical year, marked by seasons, Sabbaths, and feasts. It provides for a reading from the Torah (the first five books of the Bible) and a reading from the former or latter prophets at each service. In Palestine at the time of Jesus, these readings were arranged in a three-year cycle. In synagogue ritual the Torah scroll was carried to the lectern in procession accompanied by the singing of psalms, the appropriate reading was chanted, then the scroll was returned to its place in the ark.

In the Catholic liturgy the biblical readings are arranged in the lectionary according to seasons, Sundays, and feasts. The Sunday lectionary is a three-year cycle of three readings for each Mass. The first reading is usually from the Old Testament and usually relates thematically to the gospel selection. The second reading is generally taken from one of the New Testament letters or Revelation. The gospels of Matthew, Mark, and Luke correspond to the selections from Cycle A, B, and C, while John's gospel is read in all three cycles, especially during Lent and Easter.

The Liturgy of the Word offers a wide selection of readings from throughout the Bible. Yet, Catholics do not come to Mass for Bible study. The liturgy is not simply a history lesson or opportunity to draw out lessons from Scripture. Through the inspired Scriptures, the Lord is truly with us, speaking to us, inviting us to renew the covenant with him. The people of God have always revered Scripture as the living and powerful word of God encountered in a liturgical setting. In the liturgy we learn that God's word is still alive, powerful, and working in our world today.

For this reason, we show such profound reverence for the word of God in the Liturgy of the Word. We bind it in beautiful books; we carry it in processions with candles and incense; we proclaim it loud and clear for the whole assembly; we meditate on it and hear it interpreted for us by the wisdom of the church. We do these things because we know we are encountering Christ, the Word made flesh among us.

- Why did the early Liturgy of the Word follow the pattern of the synagogue service?

- What are some of the parallels between the liturgy of the synagogue and the Christian Liturgy of the Word?

- What are the most significant differences between the proclamation of Scripture in the church's liturgy and a communal Bible study?

LESSON 13

The Word of the Lord Spoken to Moses

LISTENING

Prepare to listen to the word of God in Scripture by lighting a candle and placing it before you. Slowly speak the words of the sacred text aloud, so that you read the text with your eyes and hear it with your ears.

Exodus 3:1–12

¹Moses was keeping the flock of his father-in-law Jethro, the priest of Midian; he led his flock beyond the wilderness, and came to Horeb, the mountain of God. ²There the angel of the LORD appeared to him in a flame of fire out of a bush; he looked, and the bush was blazing, yet it was not consumed. ³Then Moses said, "I must turn aside and look at this great sight, and see why the bush is not burned up." ⁴When the LORD saw that he had turned aside to see, God called to him out of the bush, "Moses, Moses!" And he said, "Here I am." ⁵Then he said, "Come no closer! Remove the sandals from your feet, for the place on which you are standing is holy ground." ⁶He said further, "I am the God of your father, the God of Abraham, the God of Isaac, and the God of Jacob." And Moses hid his face, for he was afraid to look at God.

⁷Then the LORD said, "I have observed the misery of my people who are in Egypt; I have heard their cry on account of their taskmasters. Indeed, I know their sufferings, ⁸and I have come down to deliver them from the Egyptians, and to bring them up out of that land to a good and broad land, a land flowing with milk and honey, to the country of the Canaanites, the Hittites, the Amorites, the Perizzites, the Hivites, and the Jebusites. ⁹The cry of the Israelites has now come to me; I have also seen how the Egyptians oppress them. ¹⁰So come, I will send you to Pharaoh to bring my people, the Israelites, out of Egypt." ¹¹But Moses said to God, "Who am I that I should go to Pharaoh, and bring the Israelites out of Egypt?" ¹²He said, "I will be with you; and this shall be the sign for you that it is I

who sent you: when you have brought the people out of Egypt, you shall worship God on this mountain."

Exodus 19:1–8

[1]On the third new moon after the Israelites had gone out of the land of Egypt, on that very day, they came into the wilderness of Sinai. [2]They had journeyed from Rephidim, entered the wilderness of Sinai, and camped in the wilderness; Israel camped there in front of the mountain. [3]Then Moses went up to God; the LORD called to him from the mountain, saying, "Thus you shall say to the house of Jacob, and tell the Israelites: [4]You have seen what I did to the Egyptians, and how I bore you on eagles' wings and brought you to myself. [5]Now therefore, if you obey my voice and keep my covenant, you shall be my treasured possession out of all the peoples. Indeed, the whole earth is mine, [6]but you shall be for me a priestly kingdom and a holy nation. These are the words that you shall speak to the Israelites."

[7]So Moses came, summoned the elders of the people, and set before them all these words that the LORD had commanded him. [8]The people all answered as one: "Everything that the LORD has spoken we will do." Moses reported the words of the people to the LORD.

UNDERSTANDING

Continue studying these foundational Old Testament readings by exploring their understanding of God speaking to his people through his word.

In his book *The Idea of the Holy*, Rudolph Otto explores humanity's experience of the divine as the *mysterium tremendum et fascinans*, the encounter with God that is majestic and terrifying, and at the same time, fascinating and alluring. This experience of God expresses well the feelings evoked by God's revelation to Moses and the Israelites in these passages from Exodus. God speaks his word to Israel from the burning bush and from the mountain through the mediation of his servant Moses, an encounter that can only be described as an awesome mystery.

God spoke mysteriously to Moses through the bush that was burning but not consumed, a flame evoking God's holiness and passion. The transcendent, eternal God revealed his presence and his will in our space-time world through his word. God taught Moses to demonstrate reverence for God's revealing presence: "Come no closer! Remove the sandals from your feet, for the place on which you are standing is holy ground" (3:5). Moses heard God's voice, received it with obedience, and taught the Israelites the proper interior respect and external reverence that orients God's people rightly in relationship to God's word.

God revealed himself to Moses at the burning bush because God had heard his people's cry and desired to deliver them and eventually to establish them securely in their own land. God later spoke his word to Moses on the mountain for the sake of his people assembled together. God said to them, "If you obey my voice and keep my covenant, you shall be my treasured possession out of all the peoples" (19:5). God's word formed the people of Israel and made the covenant possible. When Moses spoke before the elders and the assembly, telling them all that God had spoken, the entire people responded, "Everything that the LORD has spoken we will do" (19:8). The word of the Lord formed a people responsive to his will and bonded with him in covenant.

From Moses on, God's people have always encountered the word of the Lord in a liturgical setting as an essential and central element of public worship. There God's people learn who God is as he reveals the divine being and who they are to be as his people called together in covenant. The word of the Lord reveals God's commands, his sovereign will for his people and his creation, and how his word is still alive and working in our world today.

From the Old Testament through the New and up to the present day, the people of God have always revered Scripture as the living and powerful word of God. During the Liturgy of the Word the lector reads from a book that was written two or more millennia ago and concludes by saying, "The word of the Lord." These are the texts that have come to us from human authors through the inspiration of the Holy Spirit. These are the books through which God is revealed and for which God is the primary source or divine author. These are the Scriptures that the church has preserved and guarded so that God's people could continue receiving blessings and life from them. To the lector's proclamation, "The word of the Lord," the people rightly respond, "Thanks be to God." We are truly blessed and grateful that God has been willing to reveal his presence, to speak to us, to rescue us from bondage, to share his life, and enter into the bond of covenant with us.

REFLECTING

Reflect on the meaning of God's revelation to Israel in relationship to your own experience of receiving God's word within Christ's church.

- The first reading of the Liturgy of the Word is always, with the exception of the Easter season, taken from the Old Testament. What is the reason for beginning the liturgy with a selection of literature from the old covenant?

  The apostles went to the temple for the liturgy of the word, then to a home for the liturgy of the eucharist. Their readings were from the Torah

- The manifestation of God in the book of Exodus is majestic and terrifying and, at the same time, fascinating and alluring. In what ways do I experience these qualities as God reveals himself to me in the church's worship?

  Mainly thru the eucharist,

- After the reading the lector proclaims, "The word of the Lord." How do I understand this truth about the readings? In what sense are the words that I hear the revelation of God to me? *The Lord speaks to us thru the authors. They come from the Holy Spirit*

PRAYING

Remove your shoes or sandals and spend some time speaking to the One whose voice you have heard. Respond to God who has spoken to you in the words, ideas, and images from the readings. Begin with these words and continue with your own.

- Holy God, I am reluctantly drawn to you as I both fear and desire your presence. You have heard the cry of my distress and you desire to free my life from bondage. Give me the courage to respond with Moses, "Here I am," and to listen to your word to me today.

Just sit shoeless in the presence of God and place yourself under his loving gaze. Enjoy these holy moments for as long as you wish.

ACTING

Consider ways that you might bring the words you speak in liturgy more concretely into your daily life.

- To the lector's proclamation, "The word of the Lord," I respond with God's people, "Thanks be to God." How can I better express my gratitude for inspired Scripture, both to God and to other people, bringing my liturgical words into my life experiences?

Ezra Proclaims the Torah to God's Listening People

Listening

Close off the distractions around you and enter a moment of stillness. Hear this narrative of Ezra reading from the Torah and the people of Israel humbly receiving God's word.

Nehemiah 8:1–12

When the seventh month came — the people of Israel being settled in their towns — ¹all the people gathered together into the square before the Water Gate. They told the scribe Ezra to bring the book of the law of Moses, which the LORD had given to Israel. ²Accordingly, the priest Ezra brought the law before the assembly, both men and women and all who could hear with understanding. This was on the first day of the seventh month. ³He read from it facing the square before the Water Gate from early morning until midday, in the presence of the men and the women and those who could understand; and the ears of all the people were attentive to the book of the law. ⁴The scribe Ezra stood on a wooden platform that had been made for the purpose; and beside him stood Mattithiah, Shema, Anaiah, Uriah, Hilkiah, and Maaseiah on his right hand; and Pedaiah, Mishael, Malchijah, Hashum, Hash-baddanah, Zechariah, and Meshullam on his left hand. ⁵And Ezra opened the book in the sight of all the people, for he was standing above all the people; and when he opened it, all the people stood up. ⁶Then Ezra blessed the LORD, the great God, and all the people answered, "Amen, Amen," lifting up their hands. Then they bowed their heads and worshiped the LORD with their faces to the ground. ⁷Also Jeshua, Bani, Sherebiah, Jamin, Akkub, Shabbethai, Hodiah, Maaseiah, Kelita, Azariah, Jozabad, Hanan, Pelaiah, the Levites, helped the people to understand the law, while the people remained in their places. ⁸So they read from the book, from the law of God, with interpretation. They gave the sense, so that the people understood the reading.

⁹And Nehemiah, who was the governor, and Ezra the priest and scribe, and the Levites who taught the people said to all the people, "This day is holy to the LORD your God; do not mourn or weep." For all the people wept when they heard the words of the law. ¹⁰Then he said to them, "Go your way, eat the fat and drink sweet wine and send portions of them to those for whom nothing is prepared, for this day is holy to our LORD; and do not be grieved, for the joy of the LORD is your strength." ¹¹So the Levites stilled all the people, saying, "Be quiet, for this day is holy; do not be grieved." ¹²And all the people went their way to eat and drink and to send portions and to make great rejoicing, because they had understood the words that were declared to them.

UNDERSTANDING

Continue studying this ancient liturgy from the Old Testament in order to understand the roots of the Jewish and Christian Liturgy of the Word.

The event described here in the book of Nehemiah is the clearest description in the Old Testament of the roots of both the Jewish Torah reading in the synagogue and the Christian Liturgy of the Word. It is a service centered on the liturgical proclamation of Scripture with traditional ritual elements that remain through the centuries.

When the exiles returned from Babylon and reestablished the worship of God in Jerusalem, the reading of Scripture formed the heart of their worship. On this festive occasion the community invited Ezra, a priest and scribe, to lead a service of Torah instruction, since the custody and communication of the Torah were traditional parts of the ministry of Israel's priesthood. The text emphasizes the solidarity of the community, stating no fewer than ten times that "all the people" participated. The completeness of the people is also indicated by the repeated phrase "both men and women and all who could hear with understanding" (vv. 2–3). Apparently, the ceremony was intended for the whole family: husbands, wives, and children old enough to understand. They were solemnly assembled so that they could listen to God's word and respond as God's people.

The assembly gathered with a proper acknowledgment of the roles and offices of each. The religious officials joined with Ezra on a raised platform facing the people (v. 4). In the preliminary liturgical rites, Ezra ceremonially "opened the book," or rather, unrolled the scroll (v. 5). As he did so, all the people stood up. Then Ezra offered praise and blessing to God on their behalf, thanking God for the Scriptures (v. 6). The people then responded with a double "Amen," marking their assent to Ezra's prayer, and raised their hands in praise. They then bowed deeply and worshiped God. All of these gestures reflect ancient liturgical practices, providing a worshipful and receptive setting for Ezra's proclamation of "the book of the law of Moses."

Ezra read from the Torah scroll and the Levites interpreted the text so that the people understood the meaning (v. 8). This interpretation was probably both a translation of the Hebrew scroll into the Aramaic of the people and also a commentary and explanation of the text. There is an emphasis throughout the passage on "understanding," demonstrating that the response of the people to the word of the Lord is the main interest of the liturgy. The end of the passage indicates that the people left the liturgical event with great rejoicing "because they had understood the words that were declared to them" (verse 12). As the book of Nehemiah continues, it becomes clear that this ceremony had a profound effect upon the community and led to their pledge to keep God's covenant.

The main outline of this ceremony led by Ezra in Jerusalem has the same elements as our Liturgy of the Word. It includes an initial rite of praise and prayer to God, a time of solemn listening to the written word of God, an interpretation and explanation of the Scripture, and the people's response to God. These elements have formed the primary structure both for Jewish synagogue worship and for the Christian Liturgy of the Word through the ages. Other elements that continued in Christian liturgy are the following: a distinction among the priests, the ministers of the word, and the assembly; standing as a distinctive posture for receiving the word; an elevated platform for proclaiming the word; prayers and acclamations in preparation for receiving the word; and responses from the people indicating their assent to the word.

The Christian Liturgy of the Word evolved from the ancient practices of Israel. This tradition of the word is rooted in the understanding that God truly speaks to his people, communicating his life and his will to them through the mediation of prophets and inspired writers. As the word of God became increasingly written and fixed in sacred Scripture, the people of God expressed honor for the physical presence of the sacred scrolls or holy books. From the Torah ceremony of Ezra to the proclamation of the holy gospel at Sunday Mass, God's people have stood to receive God's word and listened as the Scriptures are reverently proclaimed.

REFLECTING

Consider this ancient scene of Ezra's ministry in relationship to your own experience of hearing and receiving the word of God in liturgical worship.

- When the book of Scripture was opened, the people of Jerusalem stood up, proclaimed "Amen," lifted up their hands, and bowed their heads in worship (vv. 5–6). What are some of the signs of reverence we offer to the book of Scripture in the Mass?

  Stand up: Say Alleluia - sign of cross: mind, mouth, heart
  Answer: The Word of the Lord
  Respond to the Psalm
  Ans.: Praise be to you Lord Jesus Christ

- At the weekly Sabbath service, a section of the Torah is chanted or read, so that the entire Pentateuch (Genesis, Exodus, Leviticus, Numbers, and Deuteronomy) is liturgically proclaimed each year. Simchat Torah is the annual holiday that celebrates the completion of the year's cycle of Torah readings. How is the cyclical practice of Torah reading similar to the Christian practice of annually proclaiming the gospels?

  Sunday Mass has 3 cycles (A, B, C)

- What are some ways that this text emphasizes the importance of the people's understanding of the Torah? What are some practices that lead me to a fuller understanding of Scripture?

RAYING

Pray to God from a heart that has been changed through your reflection on this scene.

- Great God of our ancestors, you have spoken your word to your people in every age. Bless us with ears eager to hear your word and with minds and hearts desiring to understand the sacred texts.

Spend some moments in prayer asking God for a deeper hunger for his word in Scripture.

ACTING

We enhance our experience of God's word in liturgy when we study the biblical texts on our own in preparation.

- Spend some time reflecting on the Scripture readings for next Sunday's Mass. Ask yourself what God might be speaking to your life through these words. Carry these initial thoughts about these readings with you to church on Sunday and see if this preparation aids your reception of the word of the Lord.

The Liturgy of the Word in the Synagogue of Nazareth

LISTENING

Prepare to read the Scripture by asking God's Spirit to open your mind, your lips, and your heart so that you may hear God's word within this text. Listen with expectancy to the inspired gospel.

Luke 4:16–22

¹⁶When [Jesus] came to Nazareth, where he had been brought up, he went to the synagogue on the sabbath day, as was his custom. He stood up to read, ¹⁷and the scroll of the prophet Isaiah was given to him. He unrolled the scroll and found the place where it was written:

> ¹⁸"The Spirit of the Lord is upon me,
>   because he has anointed me
>   to bring good news to the poor.
> He has sent me to proclaim release to the captives
>   and recovery of sight to the blind,
>   to let the oppressed go free,
> ¹⁹to proclaim the year of the Lord's favor."

²⁰And he rolled up the scroll, gave it back to the attendant, and sat down. The eyes of all in the synagogue were fixed on him. ²¹Then he began to say to them, "Today this scripture has been fulfilled in your hearing." ²²All spoke well of him and were amazed at the gracious words that came from his mouth. They said, "Is not this Joseph's son?"

Luke 24:44–49

⁴⁴Then he said to them, "These are my words that I spoke to you while I was still with you — that everything written about me in the law of Moses, the prophets, and the psalms must be fulfilled." ⁴⁵Then he opened their minds to understand the scriptures, ⁴⁶and he said to them, "Thus it is written, that the Messiah is to suffer and to rise from the dead on the third day, ⁴⁷and that repentance and forgiveness of sins is to be proclaimed in his name to all nations, beginning from Jerusalem. ⁴⁸You are witnesses of these things. ⁴⁹And see, I am sending upon you what my Father promised; so stay here in the city until you have been clothed with power from on high."

UNDERSTANDING

Consider what this gospel passage can teach you about the unity of Scripture and our challenge to hear Christ speaking to us in the Liturgy of the Word.

Luke's gospel offers us another glimpse of the synagogue liturgy, this time from the early days of Jesus' ministry. In the synagogue of Nazareth, Jesus was invited to read the selection from the prophets for the Sabbath service. The text was written to the Israelites by Isaiah, proclaiming the work of one anointed by God's Spirit to bring good news to the poor, sight for the blind, and freedom for the oppressed. Jesus stands to read, unrolls the scroll, proclaims the Scripture, then sits down and interprets the text in a sermon, beginning with the words, "Today this scripture passage has been fulfilled in your hearing" (4:21).

What God had once spoken through the prophets, was now being spoken by his anointed Son. God was making good on the promises of Scripture. In the "hearing" of the Son's word, the Scripture of old is fulfilled. Until this moment at Nazareth, Israel's liturgy had been one of expectation and hope: the congregation heard the Torah of Moses and the ancient prophets, and they prayed that the Messiah might come among them. In Jesus, what was hoped for and anticipated has come to pass.

Toward the end of Luke's gospel, on the evening of Christ's resurrection, Jesus taught his disciples that in his paschal mystery is the fulfillment of "the law of Moses, the prophets, and the psalms" (24:44). This is what we experience in the Liturgy of the Word at Mass. All the promises of the old covenant are brought to fulfillment in our hearing, as we share in the grace of the new covenant. This "fulfillment" does not mean that the old is overcome or superseded. Rather, the old is completed in the new; the old finds its fullness in the covenant formed in Christ. In him we see the rich continuity of God's plan of salvation and we are able to appreciate how all of salvation history points to his coming.

The readings for each Sunday's Mass follow the pattern of salvation history. They begin with the Old Testament, move to the New Testament, and culminate in the proclamation of the gospel. In each liturgy we are intentionally made to re-read and re-live the great moments of our salvation, the salvation for which we give God thanks and praise in the Mass. Though the relationships between the Old Testament readings and the gospel texts can be subtle, they are always connected so as to reveal the unity of God's saving plan from the old covenant to the new, a plan that continues in the Mass.

In the Liturgy of the Word the Scriptures are read reverently and carefully, for we believe that in the readings God speaks to his people, opening up the mystery of redemption and offering spiritual nourishment. Our experience of the biblical text can be life-transforming because we receive the Scriptures "not as a human word but as what it truly is, God's word" (1 Thes 2:13). Through the liturgical proclamation of the word of God, Jesus Christ is present in the midst of the assembly, just as surely as he is present in the sacrament of his body and blood.

To emphasize the sacredness of God's word in the Scriptures, St. Caesarius of Arles (*Sermo* 78, 2) spoke the following:

> I have this question for you, brothers and sisters. Which do you think more important — the word of God or the body of Christ? If you want to answer correctly, you must tell me that the word of God is not less important than the body of Christ! How careful we are, when the body of Christ is distributed to us, not to let any bit of it fall to the ground from our hand! But we should be just as careful not to let slip from our hearts the word of God.

REFLECTING

Meditate on the words of the gospel texts and consider how Christ uses the power of the gospel to form you as his disciple.

- In the twelfth century, Hugh of St. Victor wrote the following: "All sacred Scripture is but one book, and this one book is Christ; because all sacred Scripture speaks of Christ, and all sacred Scripture is fulfilled in Christ." How can I more fully realize the truth and effect of this statement?

- The liturgical readings show us how the old covenant is fulfilled in the new. What is the meaning of this "fulfillment" of the old by Christ? In what way is the first reading of the Mass related to the Gospel?

- The Second Vatican Council (*Dei Verbum*, 21) and the *Catechism of the Catholic Church* tell us: "The Church has always venerated the Scriptures as she venerates the Lord's Body. She never ceases to present to the faithful the bread of life, taken from the one table of God's Word and Christ's Body." How can I better participate in the Liturgy of the Word so that I might receive the blessing and life it is intended to convey?

PRAYING

Respond to God in prayer with the new understanding you have received from his word. Pray about the reality of Christ's presence in the liturgically proclaimed word of God.

- Speak your word to me, Christ Jesus. When I stand to listen to the gospel, help me to hear you speaking to me. Help me to experience your presence, your life, and your salvation through the words of your holy gospel.

Continue to pray as the Holy Spirit guides your heart.

ACTING

Christians through the ages have honored the book of Scripture by enthroning them on the altar and in their homes.

- Consider enthroning the Bible in your home as a physical reminder of the centrality of God's word for every part of your life. Simply place the open Bible on a table or stand, and take it from its throne each time you read from the Scriptures.

LESSON 16

Philip Guides the Ethiopian to Understand the Scripture

LISTENING

Ask God's Spirit to help you read this narrative of the early church. Try to capture the dedication of Philip and the open-heartedness of the Ethiopian.

Acts 8:25–38

²⁵Now after Peter and John had testified and spoken the word of the Lord, they returned to Jerusalem, proclaiming the good news to many villages of the Samaritans.

²⁶Then an angel of the Lord said to Philip, "Get up and go toward the south to the road that goes down from Jerusalem to Gaza." (This is a wilderness road.) ²⁷So he got up and went. Now there was an Ethiopian eunuch, a court official of the Candace, queen of the Ethiopians, in charge of her entire treasury. He had come to Jerusalem to worship ²⁸and was returning home; seated in his chariot, he was reading the prophet Isaiah. ²⁹Then the Spirit said to Philip, "Go over to this chariot and join it." ³⁰So Philip ran up to it and heard him reading the prophet Isaiah. He asked, "Do you understand what you are reading?" ³¹He replied, "How can I, unless someone guides me?" And he invited Philip to get in and sit beside him. ³²Now the passage of the scripture that he was reading was this:

> "Like a sheep he was led to the slaughter,
> and like a lamb silent before its shearer,
> so he does not open his mouth.
> ³³In his humiliation justice was denied him.
> Who can describe his generation?
> For his life is taken away from the earth."

³⁴The eunuch asked Philip, "About whom, may I ask you, does the prophet say this, about himself or about someone else?" ³⁵Then Philip began to speak, and starting with this scripture, he proclaimed to him the good news about Jesus. ³⁶As they were going along the road, they came to some water; and the eunuch said, "Look, here is water! What is to prevent me from being baptized?" ³⁸He commanded the chariot to stop, and both of them, Philip and the eunuch, went down into the water, and Philip baptized him.

UNDERSTANDING

Study the way that Phillip interpreted and applied the Scripture for the sake of the Ethiopian's salvation.

By divine guidance, Philip was sent to meet the Ethiopian official, who was returning home after worshiping in Jerusalem. The official had great power and authority as the queen's minister, but he did not have the power to understand the word of God. While traveling along the road, the Ethiopian was reading from a scroll of the prophet Isaiah. When Philip heard him reading aloud, as was the custom in the ancient world, he asked, "Do you understand what you are reading?" The Ethiopian replied, "How can I, unless someone guides me?" (vv. 30–31). Then he invited Philip to get in his chariot and sit beside him.

This selection from the Acts of the Apostles does not describe the entire conversation between Philip and the Ethiopian. It tells us only that "Philip began to speak, and starting with this scripture, he proclaimed to him the good news about Jesus" (verse 35). The passage that Philip explained to his host was an Old Testament text that speaks of God's Servant suffering for the sake of others. Philip must have explained in detail how this text, Isaiah 53, finds its completeness in Jesus. He is the Servant of God who was oppressed and afflicted, who poured himself out in death, and who bore the sins of many. From Jesus the disciples had learned to understand this passage as a key to finding his messianic mission throughout the ancient Scriptures. Philip continued this process of showing how all of Scripture finds its climactic purpose in the death and resurrection of Christ.

Philip not only interpreted the scroll of Isaiah for the Ethiopian, but helped him understand its significance for his own life. Philip proclaimed the good news. He developed the biblical passage in such a way that the Ethiopian was able to perceive its personal implications and accept the redemption of Jesus Christ for his own salvation. He was so convinced and moved by Philip's ministry that he was called to faith, received baptism, and became a follower of Christ.

This experience of Philip and the Ethiopian expresses well the dynamics of the Liturgy of the Word. The proclamation of Scripture and its interpretation in the homily leads to deeper understanding and ongoing conversion. We listen to Scripture not just to understand its literal meaning, but to allow the inspired text to influence our minds and hearts in such a way that it leads us to a fuller experience of Christ. Conversion in the Christian life is not just the initial moment of accepting Jesus, but the lifelong process of turning away from the life of sin and turning toward Christ and the fullness of life. The Liturgy of the Word places us in the presence of Christ, who converts our lives and leads us to salvation.

Preaching based on readings from Scripture is one of the practices the church inherited from the synagogue. The homily of the Mass is a liturgical act, an integral part of Christian worship. Its purpose is to explain the biblical texts and apply their message to the present day. It helps us to interpret Scripture and to truly hear it as God's word addressed to us in our times and circumstances.

REFLECTING

After listening carefully to the conversion of the Ethiopian through the ministry of Philip, consider what else you can learn about preaching within the context of the church's liturgy.

- Philip interpreted the Scripture for the Ethiopian in such a way that it led the official to request baptism and become a follower of Jesus. What do you suppose Philip said to the Ethiopian in addition to the information that could be obtained from a biblical commentary?

- The purpose of the homily in the liturgy is to help people hear the readings as the word of God and put them into practice. What are the characteristics of the best homilies you have heard?

- In what sense is conversion to Christ an ongoing and lifelong process? How does my participation in the Mass lead me to ongoing conversion of life?

PRAYING

Let the conversion of the Ethiopian lead you to respond in prayer to what you have heard and what you have understood.

- Suffering Servant, you were oppressed and afflicted, you poured yourself out in death, and you bore the sin of many. Turn my heart from the sin that imprisons me, and turn my life toward you and the fullness of life you offer me. Give me a desire to experience the Scriptures as the word of God that saves me and leads me to life with you.

Continue expressing the content of your heart in your own prayerful response.

ACTING

Consider how you might express gratitude and support for those people who interpret the Scriptures for you.

- Good preaching at the liturgy is the result of much personal study, reflection, and prayer. Take the time to express gratitude to the preacher at your next Sunday Mass by naming the specific aspects of the homily that were most helpful to you.

LESSON 17

Professing the Faith of the Church

LISTENING

In these verses, God's people attempt to summarize and express the essentials of their beliefs. Listen to these ancient statements of faith, realizing that you have inherited the faith of your ancestors.

Deuteronomy 26:1–11

¹When you have come into the land that the LORD your God is giving you as an inheritance to possess, and you possess it, and settle in it, ²you shall take some of the first of all the fruit of the ground, which you harvest from the land that the LORD your God is giving you, and you shall put it in a basket and go to the place that the LORD your God will choose as a dwelling for his name. ³You shall go to the priest who is in office at that time, and say to him, "Today I declare to the LORD your God that I have come into the land that the LORD swore to our ancestors to give us." ⁴When the priest takes the basket from your hand and sets it down before the altar of the LORD your God, ⁵you shall make this response before the LORD your God: "A wandering Aramean was my ancestor; he went down into Egypt and lived there as an alien, few in number, and there he became a great nation, mighty and populous. ⁶When the Egyptians treated us harshly and afflicted us, by imposing hard labor on us, ⁷we cried to the LORD, the God of our ancestors; the LORD heard our voice and saw our affliction, our toil, and our oppression. ⁸The LORD brought us out of Egypt with a mighty hand and an outstretched arm, with a terrifying display of power, and with signs and wonders; ⁹and he brought us into this place and gave us this land, a land flowing with milk and honey. ¹⁰So now I bring the first of the fruit of the ground that you, O LORD, have given me." You shall set it down before the LORD your God and bow down before the LORD your God. ¹¹Then you, together with the Levites and the aliens

who reside among you, shall celebrate with all the bounty that the LORD your God has given to you and to your house.

Ephesians 4:1–16

[1]I therefore, the prisoner in the Lord, beg you to lead a life worthy of the calling to which you have been called, [2]with all humility and gentleness, with patience, bearing with one another in love, [3]making every effort to maintain the unity of the Spirit in the bond of peace. [4]There is one body and one Spirit, just as you were called to the one hope of your calling, [5]one Lord, one faith, one baptism, [6]one God and Father of all, who is above all and through all and in all.

[7]But each of us was given grace according to the measure of Christ's gift. [8]Therefore it is said,

> "When he ascended on high he made captivity itself a captive;
> he gave gifts to his people."

[9](When it says, "He ascended," what does it mean but that he had also descended into the lower parts of the earth? [10]He who descended is the same one who ascended far above all the heavens, so that he might fill all things.) [11]The gifts he gave were that some would be apostles, some prophets, some evangelists, some pastors and teachers, [12]to equip the saints for the work of ministry, for building up the body of Christ, [13]until all of us come to the unity of the faith and of the knowledge of the Son of God, to maturity, to the measure of the full stature of Christ. [14]We must no longer be children, tossed to and fro and blown about by every wind of doctrine, by people's trickery, by their craftiness in deceitful scheming. [15]But speaking the truth in love, we must grow up in every way into him who is the head, into Christ, [16]from whom the whole body, joined and knit together by every ligament with which it is equipped, as each part is working properly, promotes the body's growth in building itself up in love.

UNDERSTANDING

Consider the ways that the people of Israel professed their communal faith and Paul's call to the church to be united in faith.

The book of Deuteronomy outlines a liturgy of thanksgiving to God to be offered by those who come into the land of God's promise. Each person is commanded to bring the first fruits of the land as an offering in the sanctuary. As the thanksgiving offering is brought before the Lord, each person must recite a "creed" confessing the faith of the community, declaring before God and one another what God has done in their behalf (Deut 26:5–10). The function of this creed within the liturgical ritual is both to express the unity of God's covenanted people and to express thanksgiving to God for his faithfulness.

This "creed" of Israel is a succinct summary of the story contained in the five books of the Torah. It identifies and expresses what matters most and is fundamental for the people's faith. It is the story of the patriarchs, the exodus, and the entry into the land. It is the memory of a suffering people, of God's rescue, and of his providential care. The heart of the matter is how God hears his people's pain, delivers them from oppression, and brings them to salvation. With these words of faith on their lips, the people of Israel offer their gifts to the Lord and bow down in his presence.

In the eucharistic liturgy, God's people profess their faith before offering their gifts. The Christian Creed expresses the faith of the church, but it is recited by each individual: "I believe in one God, the Father almighty.... I believe in one Lord Jesus Christ.... I believe in the Holy Spirit...." The Creed originated in the early church as a threefold profession made by those being baptized, accompanied by a triple immersion in baptismal waters. Later this baptismal declaration of faith was expanded into a fuller statement of faith, preserving its basic threefold structure, and was gradually introduced into the Mass.

Nicene

The creed is a concise summary of the biblical story, the history of our salvation — from the creation "of heaven and earth, of all things visible and invisible," through the Incarnation, Crucifixion, Resurrection and Ascension, all the way to Christ's coming again "to judge the living and the dead." It expresses what is most central and fundamental to the faith of the church. But the Creed is not just a rote recitation of doctrines. When we profess our belief, we express our readiness to be God's baptized, covenanted people, to live in a way that is worthy of the faith we proclaim in the eucharistic liturgy.

The liturgical use of the Creed, in both the Byzantine East and the Roman West, has always used the first person singular, "I believe" (*credo*, in Latin). The singular form reflects the baptismal usage, echoing the older Apostles' Creed, which was the baptismal profession of the Roman church, and the threefold "I do" of the interrogatory form of the baptismal pronouncement. But the use of the first person singular is certainly not individualistic, but expresses personal accountability for the faith of the community. St. Thomas Aquinas taught that the "I" in the Creed is the church, the whole body of Christ. In this sense, the use of the "I" highlights both personal responsibility for baptismal faith as well as communal identity and unity in belief.

The importance of the church's oneness is emphasized in Paul's teaching. He maintains that unity is a gift that God's Spirit has given to the church, but it is the responsibility of God's people to preserve and manifest that unity (Eph 4:3). Paul presents the theological foundation from which all unity arises, showing that the oneness of the church is rooted in the oneness of God: "There is one body and one Spirit, just as you were called to the one hope of your calling, one Lord, one faith, one baptism, one God and Father of all, who is above all and through all and in all" (Eph 4:4–6). Even though there is great diversity within the church — different gifts for a variety of ministries — the diversity within the body must contribute to "the unity of the faith" (Eph 3:13), as each part works together. Rather than allowing itself to be divided — "tossed to and fro and blown about by every wind of doctrine" — the church must preserve its unity by "speaking the truth in love" (Eph 3:14–15).

The church's liturgical Creed, the work of the Council of Nicea (AD 325) and the Council of Constantinople (AD 381), is drawn almost entirely from Scripture. Those doctrinal words that are not taken from Scripture are all definitive interpretations of Scripture in response to heretical belief in the early church. Dogmatic phrases such as "consubstantial with the Father" and "incarnate of the Virgin Mary" express the church's belief in the oneness of the Son with the Father and the reality that the Son became flesh in the womb of Mary. This kind of precise terminology was formulated by the greatest theologians of the church's early centuries and enables us to definitively express the core of biblical truth. The Creed is more than a list of beliefs, but expresses the "rule of faith" by which the church reads Scripture.

The purpose of the church's Creed is to express the unity that has been given to us by God. We profess that the oneness of the church is rooted in the oneness of God: "I believe in one God"; "I believe in one Lord"; "I believe in one, holy, catholic and apostolic church"; "I confess one baptism." The Eucharist is the church's sacrament of unity. As we speak the truth of our faith, united in the love of our eucharistic Christ, we profess, preserve, and manifest the unity to which we are called.

REFLECTING

Read the Creed slowly, conscious of the fact that you are professing the faith of your baptism, which you are responsible to preserve and manifest.

- In the liturgy of ancient Israel, each person was responsible for stating before God the beliefs of the community. In the liturgy of the church, each person expresses his or her baptismal faith with personal commitment. What difference does it make when I profess the Creed using the personal "I believe" rather than the generic "we believe"?

- Professing that the Son of God was "incarnate of the Virgin Mary" expresses a much fuller truth than to say that the Son was "born" of the Virgin Mary. What is the difference between these two expressions? Why is precise language so crucial when expressing the objective content of the Christian faith?

- The central theme of Paul's letter to the Ephesians is the church's unity. In what sense is the unity of the church a gift from God? What are some ways in which the church's members must struggle to maintain the church's unity?

PRAYING

Let Paul's writings to the Ephesians lead you to a deep desire for oneness within Christ's church.

- I believe in you, Father, Son, and Holy Spirit, and I pray that the unity of the Trinity is manifested in all your works. I praise you for creating me, redeeming me, and sanctifying me, and I pray that the calling of my baptism will be evident in the words I speak and the life I live.

Let the Spirit of unity guide and direct your continuing prayer.

ACTING

Consider what differences the doctrinal truths of the Creed make for your daily life.

- In *necessariis unitas* (In essentials unity); In *dubiis libertas* (In doubtful things liberty); In *omnibus autem caritas* (But in all things love). This is a common motto for Christian dialogue. In what sense does this slogan express the teaching of Paul that we must speak the truth in love? How can I express this teaching more fully through the things I say and do?

Voicing the Prayers of God's Faithful People

LISTENING

The early Christians prayed for the church and for the needs of its members. As you read these texts, pray for your community and trust in God's desire to hear and answer your prayers.

Ephesians 3:14–21

[14]For this reason I bow my knees before the Father, [15]from whom every family in heaven and on earth takes its name. [16]I pray that, according to the riches of his glory, he may grant that you may be strengthened in your inner being with power through his Spirit, [17]and that Christ may dwell in your hearts through faith, as you are being rooted and grounded in love. [18]I pray that you may have the power to comprehend, with all the saints, what is the breadth and length and height and depth, [19]and to know the love of Christ that surpasses knowledge, so that you may be filled with all the fullness of God.

[20]Now to him who by the power at work within us is able to accomplish abundantly far more than all we can ask or imagine, [21]to him be glory in the church and in Christ Jesus to all generations, forever and ever. Amen.

James 5:13–18

[13]Are any among you suffering? They should pray. Are any cheerful? They should sing songs of praise. [14]Are any among you sick? They should call for the elders of the church and have them pray over them, anointing them with oil in the name of the Lord. [15]The prayer of faith will save the sick, and the Lord will raise them up; and anyone who has committed sins will be forgiven. [16]Therefore confess

your sins to one another, and pray for one another, so that you may be healed. The prayer of the righteous is powerful and effective. [17]Elijah was a human being like us, and he prayed fervently that it might not rain, and for three years and six months it did not rain on the earth. [18]Then he prayed again, and the heaven gave rain and the earth yielded its harvest.

UNDERSTANDING

Continue exploring the prayers of the early Christians in order to understand the development of petitionary prayers in the church's worship.

Prayers of intercession are petitions made to God on behalf of others. This type of prayer is found throughout the biblical literature and tends to be personal, direct, and effective. Petitionary prayer is rooted in the covenant relationship between God and his people. Moses repeatedly interceded before God for the Israelites. Solomon offered a long petition at the dedication of the temple. Elijah petitioned God and his prayers were answered. The Psalms are filled with intercessions for both individual and communal needs.

In the New Testament, Jesus is the model of prayer and is found habitually at prayer throughout his ministry. He teaches his disciples to pray to the Father with confidence and persistence. In his letters Paul often includes prayers of petition for his readers and his young churches, and he frequently seeks their prayers for himself and his mission. He prays that the members of the church be strengthened by the Spirit, that they know the presence of Christ in their hearts, and that they be rooted in love and know the love of Christ (Eph 3:16–19). James taught his community to pray in suffering, in sickness, for the forgiveness of sins, and for healing (Jam 5:13–16). He urged his hearers to prayer with trusting faith like Elijah: "The prayer of the righteous is powerful and effective." "Elijah was a human being like us" (Jas 5:17), often falling prey to doubt and frustration, an ordinary man with an extraordinary God. For this reason, James says, any Christian has the same power to ask God with confidence and receive whatever is necessary for a life lived in him.

Just as the Jewish synagogue service included a series of petitionary prayers for the community, so at an early period a series of prayers for various intentions came to conclude the Liturgy of the Word in the celebration of the Eucharist. Though these prayers later disappeared from the Roman Mass, they were restored by the post-Vatican II revision of the liturgy. Since the catechumens of the church are formally dismissed before this prayer, it is sometimes called the "Prayer of the Faithful" since only those initiated into the sacraments of the church participated in the remainder of the liturgy. It is also called the Universal Prayer or General Intercessions, since the prayers petition God on behalf of people and their needs everywhere.

The intercessions conclude what has just been celebrated. Having heard and been nourished by God's word, the assembly responds by remembering and praying for the church and the world. The community exercises its baptismal priesthood (1 Pet 2:9) by praying for all people everywhere because "the joys and hopes, the grief and anguish of the people of our time, especially of those who are poor and afflicted, are the joys and hopes, the grief and anguish of the followers of Christ as well" (*Pastoral Constitution on the Church in the Modern World*, 1). The church prays not just for its own needs but for the salvation of the world, for civil authorities, for those who are oppressed by any burden, and for the local community, particularly for those who are sick or who have died.

The intercessory prayer follows a traditional pattern: the priest, standing at the presider's chair, addresses the people and invites them to prayer; the petitions are voiced by a deacon, cantor, or lector; the assembly responds to each petition with an invocation or silent prayer; and the priest offers a closing prayer. The petitions should be simple and succinct, composed freely but prudently, and express the prayer of the entire community. Essentially, the prayer becomes a powerful sign of the communion of the local assembly with all other communities and with the universal church.

REFLECTING

Think about the role of intercessory prayer in your own life and your worship with the church. Reflect on your challenge to pray "in the church and in Christ Jesus."

- Even though Paul prayed earnestly for his community, he realizes that his requests fall far short of what God is able to do, so he prays "to him who by the power at work within us is able to accomplish abundantly far more than all we can ask or imagine" (Eph 3:20). What is that power at work within the church through which God is able to accomplish marvels? How can I better join my life to that power in order to be an instrument of God in the world?

- If God already knows our needs and the needs of the world, what is the value of voicing our petitions to God? If the purpose of intercessory prayer is not to inform God of our needs, what might be some of the reasons why we are called to pray in this way?

- The General Intercessions should address matters that concern the whole church (leadership, unity, evangelization), the world (civil officials, justice, and peace), and the needs of the local community (the sick and faithful departed). Why am I responsible for praying not just for personal needs but for the salvation of the world?

PRAYING

Pray to the Father, whose power at work within us is able to accomplish abundantly far more than all we can ask or imagine.

- Merciful Father, I pray that I may be strengthened through the power of your Spirit, that Christ may dwell in my hearts through faith, and that I may always be rooted and grounded in love.

Continue praying like Paul as the love in your heart directs you.

ACTING

Let the General Intercessions of the Liturgy overflow into your daily life and teach you how to intercede for others.

- Each evening this week, voice your intercessory prayer to God, with at least one petition for the universal church, one for the world, and one for your local community and family.

Group Session Guide for Section IV

Begin with hospitality and welcome. Offer any announcements or instructions before entering the spirit of focused discussion. Discuss these questions or those of your own choosing:

1. In what ways has the church inherited the Liturgy of the Word from the worship tradition of Israel?

2. What can Moses teach you about reverence for the word of God? (Lesson 13)

3. What is significant about the fact that the first reading of the Mass is taken from the Old Testament? (Lesson 13)

4. What does Ezra's proclamation of the Torah in Jerusalem teach you about the proclamation of the word in Jewish synagogue worship? (Lesson 14)

5. What can you learn from synagogue worship that could lead you to a fuller understanding and appreciation of the liturgical reading of Scripture? (Lessons 14 and 15)

6. In what sense can we say that all Scripture speaks of Christ and all Scripture is fulfilled in Christ? (Lesson 15)

7. Why did the Ethiopian need Philip to interpret Scripture for him? Why is it so difficult to interpret Scripture alone? (Lesson 16)

8. What is the purpose of the homily in the Mass? What are the characteristics of the best homilies you have heard? (Lesson 16)

9. Why did Paul insist on the oneness of the church? In what way does the Creed create and express the church's unity? (Lesson 17)

10. What words in the Creed are difficult for you to understand or to believe? Why is precise language crucial for expressing the truths in the Creed? (Lesson 17)

11. Why is it so appropriate and important to include prayers for the universal church and for the whole world in each local celebration of the Mass? (Lesson 18)

12. After discussing this section, what can you do to better understand and appreciate the Liturgy of the Word when you participate in the Mass?

Remind group members to complete the six lessons from section V during the week ahead.

Offer prayers of thanksgiving aloud to God for the insights and understanding you gained in the lesson this week.

Offer prayers for your own needs and the needs of others. Pray for the grace to act upon any decisions or resolutions you have made during your study.

Conclude together: *Hail Mary, full of grace …*

Section V

The Liturgy of the Eucharist

The Liturgy of the Word and the Liturgy of the Eucharist form an inseparable unity and a single act of worship. Our encounter with God through his word in Scripture leads us to the altar of Christ's sacrifice. In the word proclaimed at Mass, we enter into the saving mystery that God has accomplished for us throughout history, and in the sacrament of the altar we participate in the new covenant and join our lives with the Word made flesh. Through the church's liturgy, in word and sacrament, we take our place in God's saving history and enter the paschal mystery.

While the Liturgy of the Word focuses on the table of the Lord's word — the ambo (or lectern) — the Liturgy of the Eucharist centers on the altar — both as a place of sacrifice and as a table from which we are fed. The eucharistic action at the altar may rightly be called both a holy sacrifice and a sacred meal. It is our participation in the once-for-all sacrifice of Christ on the cross and our sharing in the sacrificial banquet that completes the covenant and gives us eternal life.

The church has arranged the entire Liturgy of the Eucharist in parts corresponding to the very words and actions of Christ: taking, giving thanks, breaking, and sharing. For he took the bread and the chalice, he gave thanks, he broke the bread, and gave it to his disciples, saying, "Take, eat, and drink: this is my body; this is the cup of my blood. Do this in memory of me." At the Preparation of the Gifts, the bread and the wine are brought to the altar, the same elements that Christ took into his hands. In the Eucharistic Prayer, the church gives thanks to God for the whole work of salvation, and the offerings become the body and blood of Christ. Through the Fraction and through Communion, the faithful receive the Lord's body and blood in the same way Christ gave them to his apostles.

Our routine participation in the Mass can tend to blunt our appreciation of all that the Liturgy of the Eucharist involves. Taking time to understand it more deeply and reflect on its many dimensions can enhance our active and conscious participation. Eucharistic worship requires that we cultivate a liturgical consciousness, the inward assurance that in the sacred mysteries we have communion with the living God and draw life from him. Our culture today is dominated by a materialistic worldview. Confident in human autonomy and self-sufficiency, it rejects the reality of sin and denies any need for supernatural salvation. In contrast, a Christian worldview teaches us that the world needs God and has a Savior who can free us from the bondage of sin and death. In the midst of a culture unable to see any reality beyond the visible world, the mysteries of the Christian faith offer good news for the world and promise victory over the forces of evil, futility, and death.

A eucharistic spirituality enables us to face the blindness of our culture with the vision of believers. It instills within us dependence on our Creator, the humble recognition that we owe thanksgiving to God for every good gift. It enables us to know, through sacramental signs and supernatural faith, that earth touches heaven in our worship, that the angels and saints are with us, that we receive the true body and blood of our once dead and now risen Lord, that we are sons and daughters of God called to share the fullness of life. The Eucharist inspires us with a beautiful vision of life. It gives us zeal for the evangelization and sanctification of our world, deepens our desire to make our lives a holy offering to God, and shows us our role in God's redemptive plan for the world in which all things will be reconciled in Christ, and every knee in heaven and on earth shall bend in worship.

- In what sense do the Liturgy of the Word and the Liturgy of the Eucharist form a single act of worship?

  The L of the word takes us to the altar, the holy sacrifice which leads us to eternal life,

- How do the words and actions of Jesus — taking, giving thanks, breaking, and sharing — form the primary parts of the Liturgy of the Eucharist?

- Why is it so difficult to cultivate a eucharistic spirituality in our culture today?

  Our culture has so many distractions

Presenting the Gifts of Bread and Wine

LISTENING

Consider the sacrificial offerings of the ancient priest Melchizedek, and then hear the New Testament letters teach about the living sacrifices of our lives that we present to God. Let these sacrificial texts lead you to ponder your offerings at the altar.

Genesis 14:18–20

[18]And King Melchizedek of Salem brought out bread and wine; he was priest of God Most High. [19]He blessed him and said,

> "Blessed be Abram by God Most High,
>   maker of heaven and earth;
> [20]and blessed be God Most High,
>   who has delivered your enemies into your hand!"

And Abram gave him one tenth of everything.

Romans 12:1–2

[1]I appeal to you therefore, brothers and sisters, by the mercies of God, to present your bodies as a living sacrifice, holy and acceptable to God, which is your spiritual worship. [2]Do not be conformed to this world, but be transformed by the renewing of your minds, so that you may discern what is the will of God — what is good and acceptable and perfect.

1 Peter 2:4–5, 9–10

[4]Come to him, a living stone, though rejected by mortals yet chosen and precious in God's sight, and [5]like living stones, let yourselves be built into a spiritual house, to be a holy priesthood, to offer spiritual sacrifices acceptable to God through Jesus Christ.

⁹But you are a chosen race, a royal priesthood, a holy nation, God's own people, in order that you may proclaim the mighty acts of him who called you out of darkness into his marvelous light.

¹⁰Once you were not a people,
but now you are God's people;
once you had not received mercy,
but now you have received mercy.

UNDERSTANDING

Try to better understand the meaning of the bread and wine you present for offering in the Mass, and seek to comprehend the priestly ministry you share as a baptized member of Christ's body.

Melchizedek is the first priest mentioned in the Bible. He is a "priest of God Most High," and also the King of Salem, a land that would later be called "Jeru-salem" (Ps 76:2). We see this combination of priest and king applied to the royal son of David (Psalm 110:4), and in the New Testament to Jesus (Hebrews 7). Melchizedek's sacrifice involved no animal offering. Rather, he brought bread and wine as a thanksgiving offering to God, which the early Christians understood to be an anticipation of the Eucharist.

Under the old covenant, the people provided the priest with the substance of the sacrifice. For example, people would pick a lamb from their flock, representing the best of their labor, and bring it to the temple for sacrifice. The priest would receive the offering and sacrifice it on behalf of those offering it. In the Mass, the action is similar. The congregation presents the offerings of bread and wine, usually in the form of a procession, to the ministers at the altar. Other gifts may also be presented, such as a monetary collection or food for the poor. These gifts represent, as they did under the old covenant, all the prayers and good works, the joys and sufferings of God's people.

Paul urged all followers of Jesus to present their whole lives as an offering to God: "Present your bodies as a living sacrifice, holy and acceptable to God, which is your spiritual worship" (Rom 12:1). In all the circumstances of life — our home, work, family, friends, as well as explicitly religious activities and Christian outreach — we lift up our lives as a living sacrifice, giving ourselves and all that we do to God, to live our lives for God's honor and glory.

In the ancient church, the bread and wine were often personally supplied by members of the faithful. Although today these gifts are usually purchased with our monetary offerings, they still represent our personal contribution, our presentation to the Lord. The bread and wine that we bring to the altar embody the spiritual worship of our lives. It is an external act that represents our internal self-gift to God, which will be offered with Christ in the Eucharistic Prayer. The physical elements of bread and wine and the spiritual offering of ourselves are our means of participating in the sacrifice of the Mass.

The people of God offer their lives as spiritual sacrifices represented by the bread and wine by virtue of their common priesthood, sometimes called the baptismal priesthood. The whole church is a priestly people. Through baptism, all the faithful share in the priesthood of Christ. As living stones, we become the temple, and by offering living sacrifices, we share a priesthood (1 Pet 2:4–5). Though this baptismal priesthood is different than the ministerial priesthood, we inherit the dignity of God's people under the old covenant: "You are a chosen race, a royal priesthood, a holy nation, God's own people (1 Pet 2:9). This baptismal priesthood engages us actively in the sacrifice taking place at the altar. When we consciously unite their own sacrifices with the sacrifice of the Mass, the calling, efforts, and sufferings of our daily lives take on a whole new realm of effectiveness, power, and meaning.

The prayers offered at the altar are Jewish blessing prayers to God the Creator: "Through your goodness we have received the bread we offer you… the wine we offer you." The prayers acknowledge the elements of the earth, made into bread and wine through the "work of human hands." Though they are imperfect offerings, we ask that they be taken up into the perfect sacrifice of Christ and returned to us as "the bread of life" and "our spiritual drink" to nourish our lives with Christ himself. In this way, the imperfect sacrifices of the faithful are sanctified and perfected. What we offer as natural becomes supernatural. What begins as a human effort becomes a divine gift.

After the priest has prepared the altar for Eucharist, he invites the assembly to pray "that my sacrifice and yours may be acceptable to God, the almighty Father." The priest reminds the people that that they, too, offer the sacrifice of their lives. At the hands of the ordained priest, the lives of all God's people are offered up in submission and thanksgiving to God. In response to the priest's invitation, the people reply: "May the Lord accept the sacrifice at your hands for the praise and glory of his name, for our good and the good of all his holy Church." It is only by joining ourselves to Christ, the perfect sacrifice, that the contribution of our living, spiritual sacrifices can be truly acceptable to the Father and a means of sanctifying the world.

REFLECTING

Spend some time meditating on the gifts of bread and wine and how they express your offering. Consider the offerings of your own life and how God multiplies their effectiveness in union with the sacrifice of Christ.

- The ritual of carrying up the gifts connects us with the tradition of the early church in which people brought up the bread and wine that they had worked to prepare for the Eucharist. What further meaning have I learned about the symbolic significance of the gifts of bread and wine?

- Consider the gospel account of the multiplication of the loaves and fish, which is a prefiguration of the Eucharist. In the priestly action of uniting our efforts with Christ's sacrifice, our daily prayers, works, joys, and sufferings are multiplied and given real power for the sanctification of the world. How does the gospel miracle help me understand the Eucharist?

- Through the Eucharist, Christ sanctifies our imperfect works and makes them whole and supernaturally effective. In what way does this help me understand the Catholic belief that my good works have a role in my salvation?

PRAYING

Pray to God, who knows you intimately, cares about you deeply, and accepts you unconditionally.

- Blessed are you, Lord God of all creation, for through your goodness we present to you our very lives represented by the gifts of bread and wine. I ask you to take my cares and worries, my sufferings and prayers, and join them to the perfect sacrifice of Christ for the salvation of the world.

After the altar is prepared, the priest may incense the altar and the gifts as a sign of the church's offering and prayer rising like incense in the sight of God. Imagine your prayers rising like incense before God.

ACTING

Consider how you might more consciously integrate your daily life and your Sunday worship.

- All that we do — in the liturgy and in our lives in the world — is meant to be in the service of consecrating this world to God. How can I more consciously unite my life to Christ so that my daily works may take on more power, meaning, and effectiveness for God's kingdom?

LESSON 20

Holy, Holy, Holy is the Lord of Hosts

LISTENING

The threefold "Holy" was chanted in the earthly temple of Jerusalem and is sung forever in the heavenly temple. Unite your words and your praise with ancient Israel and with the hosts of heaven.

Isaiah 6:1–4

¹In the year that King Uzziah died, I saw the Lord sitting on a throne, high and lofty; and the hem of his robe filled the temple. ²Seraphs were in attendance above him; each had six wings: with two they covered their faces, and with two they covered their feet, and with two they flew. ³And one called to another and said:

"Holy, holy, holy is the LORD of hosts;
the whole earth is full of his glory."

⁴The pivots on the thresholds shook at the voices of those who called, and the house filled with smoke. ⁵And I said: "Woe is me! I am lost, for I am a man of unclean lips, and I live among a people of unclean lips; yet my eyes have seen the King, the LORD of hosts!"

Matthew 21:8–11

⁸A very large crowd spread their cloaks on the road, and others cut branches from the trees and spread them on the road. ⁹The crowds that went ahead of him and that followed were shouting,

"Hosanna to the Son of David!
Blessed is the one who comes in the name of the Lord!
Hosanna in the highest heaven!"

¹⁰When he entered Jerusalem, the whole city was in turmoil, asking, "Who is this?" ¹¹The crowds were saying, "This is the prophet Jesus from Nazareth in Galilee."

Revelation 4:1–8

¹After this I looked, and there in heaven a door stood open! And the first voice, which I had heard speaking to me like a trumpet, said, "Come up here, and I will show you what must take place after this." ²At once I was in the spirit, and there in heaven stood a throne, with one seated on the throne! ³And the one seated there looks like jasper and carnelian, and around the throne is a rainbow that looks like an emerald. ⁴Around the throne are twenty-four thrones, and seated on the thrones are twenty-four elders, dressed in white robes, with golden crowns on their heads. ⁵Coming from the throne are flashes of lightning, and rumblings and peals of thunder, and in front of the throne burn seven flaming torches, which are the seven spirits of God; ⁶and in front of the throne there is something like a sea of glass, like crystal.

Around the throne, and on each side of the throne, are four living creatures, full of eyes in front and behind: ⁷the first living creature like a lion, the second living creature like an ox, the third living creature with a face like a human face, and the fourth living creature like a flying eagle. ⁸And the four living creatures, each of them with six wings, are full of eyes all around and inside. Day and night without ceasing they sing,

"Holy, holy, holy,
the Lord God the Almighty,
who was and is and is to come."

UNDERSTANDING

After listening to these songs of praise from heaven and earth, consider their meaning and context within the Preface of the Eucharistic Prayer.

The Eucharistic Prayer begins with a dialogue between celebrant and people that makes clear the central purpose of the whole prayer. The celebrant extends the invitation: "Lift up your hearts." We are invited to raise our hearts — our thoughts, desires, and sentiment — to the realm of God. In the Mass, the priest speaks and acts *in persona Christi capitis* (in the person of Christ, the head of his body). Our response, "We lift them up to the Lord," expresses our joyful desire to enter heaven and join our voices with the angels and saints in prayers of thanks to our God. This is not just a nice expression of feeling and imagination. As with all other parts of the Mass, there is a sacramental realism at work. Our feet may still be planted in our parish church, but our liturgy on earth is part of the eternal heavenly liturgy.

In the book of Revelation, John the seer is invited by a voice in heaven to "Come up here" (Rev 4:1). Like him, we are welcomed into the assembly in which all creation worships God. Revelation shows us that in the end there is truly only one liturgy, the one in heaven. There is only one altar, the one in heaven. There is only one high priest, Jesus in heaven. Our liturgy on earth is part of the eternal heavenly liturgy where we praise God with myriads of angels and saints beyond number.

The dialogue between celebrant and people introduces the Preface (*Praefatio* in Latin, meaning "proclamation" rather than "introduction"), which should be chanted or stated in a persuasive and convincing voice. The text changes based on the liturgical season or feast, but it always sets forth a particular reason for praising God on this occasion. The various prefaces recall for us the entire biblical story, giving thanks to God for creation and the whole history of redemption, which reached its summit in the death and resurrection of Jesus Christ.

The Preface always concludes in a way that invites us to join the angels and saints in praising God's glory with one voice. The acclamation of praise, the thrice-repeated "Holy" (*Sanctus* in Latin), is sung or said by the whole congregation. This ancient hymn is derived from Isaiah's vision of the winged seraphim praising God in the temple: "Holy, holy, holy is the LORD of hosts; the whole earth is full of his glory" (Isa 6:3). This Trishagion (Thrice Holy) is the Hebrew superlative: God alone is holy and transcendent above all others. "The LORD of hosts" (Isa 6:3, 5) is a divine title that proclaims God as King of Zion with hosts of angels at his command. The "glory" that fills the whole earth is God's majestic splendor made known in his creation, the outward manifestation of his holiness. This song of praise from the heavenly liturgy probably reflects an acclamation sung in Jerusalem's temple, with swirling incense filling the sacred space.

This praise of God was extended in the Christian liturgy to include the words of praise given to Jesus as he entered Jerusalem: "Blessed is the one who comes in the name of the Lord! Hosanna in the highest heaven!" (Matt 21:9). The words are from a psalm that pilgrims to Jerusalem would sing at Passover (Ps 118:25–26). The Hebrew word *hosanna* essentially means "save us, we pray." It is an appeal that the Jews raised to God begging for intervention and mercy. For Christians, *hosanna* is the recognition that Jesus is the Messiah and Lord, and it is a cry for our own salvation.

The Sanctus entered the liturgy in the ancient church. Clement of Rome indicates that the Christians sang some version of the hymn already in the first century. It appeared in some Eastern liturgies by the third century and eventually found its way into nearly every rite. As we chant the acclamation, we join our voices with those of heaven and with the church throughout the centuries, entering with the eyes of faith into the majestic and awesome presence of God.

REFLECTING

Meditate on the liturgical dialogue that lifts our hearts to heaven and enables us to sing of God's glory with the angels and saints.

- In the opening dialogue of the Eucharistic Prayer, the people respond, "It is right and just" following the invitation, "Let us give thanks to the Lord our God." The declaration, "It is right and just," reminds us that it is not only a good thing to give God thanks, but it is our duty and responsibility as his creatures to do so. In what ways do I understand that giving thanks to God is a right, a privilege, and a responsibility?

  Our duty & salvation, always & every where to give you thanks Lord, Holy Father, almighty & merciful Father thru Christ our Lord. We should be in awe of Christ & God – glad that he considers us worthy of adoring him.

- Isaiah's experience of God's holiness gave the prophet a humble sense of his own inadequacy and changed the direction of his life. In what ways might an experience of God's awesome majesty and transcendent holiness lead to a person's internal change?

  When you realize God's "awesome majesty" you wonder why he even bothers with you! This urges one to do better.

- We sing about the hosts of angels in some popular Christmas carols: the first verse of "Hark! The Herald Angels Sing" announces, "with th'angelic host proclaim, 'Christ is born in Bethlehem,'" and the second verse of "Silent Night" declares, "Heav'nly hosts sing alleluia; Christ, the Savior, is born!" How does it affect my sense of God's presence and my participation in liturgy to sing that God is the "Lord God of hosts"?

  I am just one person among all who are constantly praising God all over the world (at every mass). I have a lot of company which makes it more awesome.

PRAYING

Join your prayer with the entire church as you acclaim God's glory and give him thanks.

- It is truly right and just, our duty and salvation, always and everywhere to give you thanks, Father most holy, through your beloved Son, Jesus Christ, for you are the one God living and true, existing before all ages and abiding for all eternity.

Continue pouring out your prayer until words are no longer necessary or useful. Then simply rest in the divine presence, contemplating the majestic holiness of God.

ACTING

Try to adopt some of the church's liturgical prayers in your own private practice of prayer.

- Remind yourself each day to "lift up your heart." Let this practice give you hope and confidence as it reminds you that you are united with the prayers of the church in heaven and throughout the world.

Jesus' Prayer of Consecration to the Father

LISTENING

This prayer of Jesus to the Father at the Last Supper is sometimes called Jesus' high priestly prayer or his prayer of consecration. Call upon the Holy Spirit to fill your heart and guide your careful reading.

John 17:1–26

[1][Jesus] looked up to heaven and said, "Father, the hour has come; glorify your Son so that the Son may glorify you, [2]since you have given him authority over all people, to give eternal life to all whom you have given him. [3]And this is eternal life, that they may know you, the only true God, and Jesus Christ whom you have sent. [4]I glorified you on earth by finishing the work that you gave me to do. [5]So now, Father, glorify me in your own presence with the glory that I had in your presence before the world existed.

[6]"I have made your name known to those whom you gave me from the world. They were yours, and you gave them to me, and they have kept your word. [7]Now they know that everything you have given me is from you; [8]for the words that you gave to me I have given to them, and they have received them and know in truth that I came from you; and they have believed that you sent me. [9]I am asking on their behalf; I am not asking on behalf of the world, but on behalf of those whom you gave me, because they are yours. [10]All mine are yours, and yours are mine; and I have been glorified in them. [11]And now I am no longer in the world, but they are in the world, and I am coming to you. Holy Father, protect them in your name that you have given me, so that they may be one, as we are one. [12]While I was with them, I protected them in your name that you have given me. I guarded them, and not one of them was lost except the one destined to be

lost, so that the scripture might be fulfilled. [13]But now I am coming to you, and I speak these things in the world so that they may have my joy made complete in themselves. [14]I have given them your word, and the world has hated them because they do not belong to the world, just as I do not belong to the world. [15]I am not asking you to take them out of the world, but I ask you to protect them from the evil one. [16]They do not belong to the world, just as I do not belong to the world. [17]Sanctify them in the truth; your word is truth. [18]As you have sent me into the world, so I have sent them into the world. [19]And for their sakes I sanctify myself, so that they also may be sanctified in truth.

[20]"I ask not only on behalf of these, but also on behalf of those who will believe in me through their word, [21]that they may all be one. As you, Father, are in me and I am in you, may they also be in us, so that the world may believe that you have sent me. [22]The glory that you have given me I have given them, so that they may be one, as we are one, [23]I in them and you in me, that they may become completely one, so that the world may know that you have sent me and have loved them even as you have loved me. [24]Father, I desire that those also, whom you have given me, may be with me where I am, to see my glory, which you have given me because you loved me before the foundation of the world.

[25]"Righteous Father, the world does not know you, but I know you; and these know that you have sent me. [26]I made your name known to them, and I will make it known, so that the love with which you have loved me may be in them, and I in them."

UNDERSTANDING

Try to understand the light that this final prayer of Jesus before his passion shines on the eucharistic worship of his church.

John's gospel presents these words of Jesus as his final prayer at table with his disciples before his passion. Jesus lifts his eyes toward heaven and addresses God as "Father." He commits his imminent death into God's hands and prays that his own glorification — his crucifixion, death, resurrection, and exaltation — will give glory to the Father (vv. 1–5). In this glorification of the Father and the Son, those in his church have "eternal life," the fullness of life that God has brought into human existence, to be lived not just after death but in the present.

Addressing God as "Holy Father," Jesus shows that his relationship with the Father becomes the pattern and source of the disciples' relationship with himself. He prays that his disciples may be united as one, just as he and the Father are one (v. 11). As the Father has sent Jesus into the world, so Jesus sends the disciples into the world for

God's service (v. 18). And Jesus prays for God to sanctify the disciples, making them holy as Jesus is holy (v. 19). The purpose of Jesus' self-sacrifice is that the disciples, too, may be consecrated, made holy for their redemptive mission in the world.

The vision of Jesus transcends the present moment at table with his disciples and extends into his mission for the world. He prays not just for those who share the Last Supper with him, but for his whole church, all those who will believe through their word (v. 20). He prays for a church taken into the unity of God, united in its divine mission: "As you, Father, are in me and I am in you, may they also be in us" (v. 21). And finally, Jesus prays that all might know the love the Father has bestowed upon him and be swept up into the love that unites the Father and the Son. Through this mutual indwelling, the church may be united in love and may continually make God known to the world (vv. 22–24). At this moment of Jesus' final, consummate act of love for the world, Jesus knows that he is offering himself so that God's love may be fully revealed. In this way, Jesus says, God's love may be in the people of his church and Jesus himself may be in them (v. 26).

In the Eucharistic Prayer, God's saving actions, accomplished in Christ, are remembered, not as past events, but as events that continue to accomplish their effects here and now. Within the sacramental worldview of Jesus and the church, remembering (*anamnesis* in Greek) is a much stronger action than in our culture. It is not just recalling the past, but making the past, with all of its saving power, present in our midst. In celebrating the Eucharist, the church is fulfilling Jesus' command to keep his memorial: "Do this in memory of me." It does this by remembering his blessed passion, glorious resurrection, and ascension to the Father. Thus, in the Liturgy of the Eucharist, we see the culmination of biblical history right in front of us on the altar.

In this memorial, the church joins in Christ's self-offering to the Father in the Holy Spirit. It calls the people of God not only to offer Christ as the perfect victim but also to learn to offer themselves. In doing so they are drawn into ever more perfect unity, through Christ's mediation, with the Father and with one another, so that at last God may be all in all. They, too, are consecrated, swept up into the loving union of the Father and the Son, and made holy for their redemptive mission in the world.

The intercessions that follow give expression to the fact that the Eucharist is celebrated in communion with the entire church, of heaven as well as of earth, and that the offering is made for the church and all its members, living and dead, who have been called to participate in the redemption and the salvation purchased by Christ's body and blood. Thus, in the Eucharistic Prayer all of God's creation is brought together — from the angels to the good things of the earth, from the entire communion of saints to the assembly gathered at the altar. Listen to Eucharistic Prayer II: "Humbly we pray that, partaking of the Body and Blood of Christ, we may be gathered into one by the Holy Spirit."

REFLECTING

- Jesus tells his disciples that the result of his consummate act of love is to make them a holy offering to God: "I sanctify myself, so that they also may be sanctified in truth" (v. 19). Though most of the time we consider that Jesus is our sacrifice to God, how often do I consider that Jesus' sacrifice enables me to join my life to his to make my life a consecrated sacrifice to God? What are the practical results of such a consideration?

  This brings us closer to God the Father.

- Throughout salvation history, God's universal presence became increasingly personal and interior in his people. In his final prayer at table, Jesus declared to the Father that he would offer himself fully on the cross so that he would dwell within believers: "so that the love with which you have loved me may be in them, and I in them" (v. 26). The eucharistic sacrifice is the final step in the long path of God's "descent" into the human condition: creation, revelation, incarnation ("with them"), Eucharist ("in them"). How is Christ's eucharistic presence in me able to transform my life?

  God considered me worthy enough to take part in the eucharist, therefore I feel I must live a life worth of Gods trust in me.

- The Bible leads us to the Mass. In the Liturgy of the Eucharist, we fulfill the command of Christ: "Do this in memory of me." In what sense do we experience the culmination of biblical history enacted before us on the altar?

PRAYING

Respond to God's word to you with your own words to God. Speak from your heart in response to the insights you have received.

- Holy Father, we give you thanks that you have held us worthy to minister in your presence. As we offer to you the bread of life and the chalice of salvation, we pray that our lives will become a consecrated offering to you and that we will be gathered into the unity and love you share with your Son, our Lord Jesus Christ.

In contemplative silence, ask to experience God's divine love through the work of the Holy Spirit within you.

ACTING

Consider the practical implications of Christ's prayer of consecration for your life.

- The Eucharist is the sacrament of unity, joining God's people on earth and in heaven, uniting the church throughout the world, and unifying the assembly in Christ by the Holy Spirit. How can I experience this unity more fully? What does this sacrament of unity practically demand of me?

The Institution of Eucharistic Worship

▌LISTENING

Listen to these words, united with all the people throughout the world and through the centuries who have heard these enduring words of Jesus. Read the passages slowly and carefully, asking God's Spirit to help you read these familiar passages anew.

Matthew 26:26–30

²⁶While they were eating, Jesus took a loaf of bread, and after blessing it he broke it, gave it to the disciples, and said, "Take, eat; this is my body." ²⁷Then he took a cup, and after giving thanks he gave it to them, saying, "Drink from it, all of you; ²⁸for this is my blood of the covenant, which is poured out for many for the forgiveness of sins. ²⁹I tell you, I will never again drink of this fruit of the vine until that day when I drink it new with you in my Father's kingdom."

³⁰When they had sung the hymn, they went out to the Mount of Olives.

Luke 22:14–20

¹⁴When the hour came, he took his place at the table, and the apostles with him. ¹⁵He said to them, "I have eagerly desired to eat this Passover with you before I suffer; ¹⁶for I tell you, I will not eat it until it is fulfilled in the kingdom of God." ¹⁷Then he took a cup, and after giving thanks he said, "Take this and divide it among yourselves; ¹⁸for I tell you that from now on I will not drink of the fruit of the vine until the kingdom of God comes." ¹⁹Then he took a loaf of bread, and when he had given thanks, he broke it and gave it to them, saying, "This is my body, which is given for you. Do this in remembrance of me." ²⁰And he did the same with the cup after supper, saying, "This cup that is poured out for you is the new covenant in my blood."

UNDERSTANDING

Seek to understand the full meaning of these texts in the context of the gospels and the eucharistic liturgies of the church throughout the centuries.

The gospels of Matthew, Mark, and Luke place the Last Supper on the eve of the Passover, in which Jesus would sacrifice his life for the life of the world. As the Passover meal personally connects each new generation of Jews to their liberation from slavery, the Eucharist connects the followers of Jesus with his liberating victory over sin and death. Jesus transformed the ancient Passover supper into the sacrament whereby people of all times may enter into the redemption that he accomplished for us on the cross.

The institution of the eucharistic sacrifice presents Jesus not as the passive victim of a tragic crucifixion, but the active hero who gives his life for others. The words and actions of Jesus over the bread and wine transform the Last Supper from the final meal of a doomed prisoner to a sacrament of self-giving and generous love. The dying Servant of the Lord gave his own body and blood, his very self, so that all might live.

Jesus' words, "blood of the covenant" (Matt 26:28), are an excerpt from the covenant at Sinai, when Moses splattered the blood of the sacrifice on the altar and the people (Exod 24:5–8). The sacrifice ratified the bond between God and his people, and the blood expressed the sharing of all the people in the life of the victim. The sacrificial animals of the ancient covenant were neither divine nor human, but now the covenant is ratified in the blood of Jesus, who is both human and divine. He is the perfect sacrifice "which is poured out for many for the forgiveness of sins." All who drink the eucharistic cup participate in the blood of the covenant, are redeemed from bondage, and are forgiven of sins.

The sacrifice of Jesus was quite different from the sacrifices of old. While the blood of the animal victim was offered to God in atonement for human sins under the old covenant, the sacrifice of Jesus, made present in the Eucharist, is a personal act of mercy. Twice in Matthew's gospel Jesus had quoted the word of the Lord through the prophet Hosea: "I desire mercy, not sacrifice" (Matt 9:13; 12:7; Hos 6:6). God desires a personal response, not just the offering of animal victims. Jesus showed mercy to sinners through shedding his blood and offering it for the forgiveness of sins. In Luke's gospel, Jesus states, "This cup that is poured out for you is the new covenant in my blood" (Luke 22:20). The "new covenant," foretold by God through the prophet Jeremiah, would be written on the hearts of God's people: "For I will forgive their iniquity and remember their sin no more" (Jer 31:33–34). This new covenant in Jesus is rooted in God's mercy and forgiveness. As Jesus accepted for himself the cup of suffering and death, he passed on to us the cup of forgiveness and life.

Like all farewell discourses in the Bible, this narrative of the Last Supper is written to address future generations. Standing at the beginning of the passion accounts of each gospel, this discourse of Jesus interprets the saving events of his dying and rising, showing future Christians how to enter into his paschal mystery. He tells them, "Do this in remembrance of me" (Luke 22:19), which means not only performing the ritual and making present again the saving actions of Christ, but also making the same self-gift that Jesus made. The broken body "given for you" and the cup "poured out for you" (Luke 22:19–20) is the body and blood of Christ, but in the Eucharist it is also that of the church, uniting itself with the offering of Christ and giving itself as the sacrament of Christ's presence in the world.

This final discourse of Jesus shows how the Christian Eucharist not only brings the saving moments of the past into the present, but also how the Eucharist anticipates the future. Jesus states that he will not eat the meal or drink the fruit of the vine until it is fulfilled in the kingdom of God (Matt 26:29; Luke 22:16, 18). In fact, this kingdom of God began with the apostolic church after the resurrection, and it looks forward to perfect completion in the last days. Jesus appeared to chosen witnesses as they celebrated the Eucharist with him (Luke 24:30; Acts 10:41). Though the fullness of God's kingdom will not come until the final banquet at the end of time, in the eucharistic celebrations of the church the kingdom is present with Jesus. The church that prays "thy kingdom come" also celebrates the presence of the risen Christ in its Eucharist.

This tradition about what Jesus did and said at the Last Supper became the heart of the church's Eucharist. In the context of the Mass, these words of institution are not just a historical narrative but the means by which the church carries out Jesus' command to perpetuate the eucharistic sacrifice. As the priest speaks in the person of Christ, pronouncing the blessing over the gifts of bread and wine, we receive the body and blood of Christ and participate in his triumph over sin and death.

REFLECTING

Reflect on the words of institution from the gospels and their enactment in the Eucharistic Prayer. Be grateful that Jesus left his apostles the command to perpetuate his words and actions.

- The words and actions of Jesus at the Last Supper changed his last meal with his disciples into an everlasting sacrament of love. What are the primary words and gestures of Jesus that gave the Eucharist this meaning?

  This is my body. This is my blood which is poured out.

- Isaiah's song of the Servant says, "He poured out himself to death ... yet he bore the sins of many." This use of "many" enters into the institution narrative of the gospels in which Jesus says his blood is "poured out for many" (Matt 26:28; Mark 14:24). The expression "for many" in the words of institution is derived from a Hebrew way of expressing a vast multitude. Why has the Institution Narrative of the Mass always said "*pro multis*" (for many) rather than "*pro omnibus*" (for all)?

  It only affects those who believe + are present. God gave us freedom of choice & not everyone chooses to believe.

- The "many" are those who become part of the covenant that Christ's sacrifice creates, the community of salvation who will inherit the kingdom of God. While Christ died for all (2 Cor 5:14–15; 1 John 2:2) and God desires everyone to be saved (1 Tim 2:4), only those who accept the gift of salvation are numbered among the "many" to whom the text refers. In what way do the words of eucharistic consecration express the necessity of my participation in the mystery of salvation as well as the graciousness of God's gift?

  He basically command us to; Take, eat Drink from it.

PRAYING

After pondering the Institution Narrative of the Mass, respond to God in prayer.

- Lord Jesus, you invited your disciples to experience the saving mysteries of your death and resurrection for all times by celebrating the Eucharist. As your body is given up and your blood poured out for me, renew your covenant within me so that I may unite my life in union with yours and give my life for others.

Continue offering your prayer to God with the words, ideas, and images from your listening to the Scripture.

ACTING

Consider your own responsibility in accepting and receiving the salvation God offers you.

- Though Christ is the atoning sacrifice for the sins of the whole world, each person must participate in the mystery of salvation. How can I better receive the gift of supernatural life and participate in the salvation God offers me?

LESSON 23

A Pure Offering to God among All the Nations

LISTENING

Hear the ancient yet ever-new voice of God speaking to you through the words of the Scriptures. Prepare for the new understandings and insights these inspired writings will offer to you.

2 Chronicles 7:1–4

¹When Solomon had ended his prayer, fire came down from heaven and consumed the burnt offering and the sacrifices; and the glory of the LORD filled the temple. ²The priests could not enter the house of the LORD, because the glory of the LORD filled the LORD's house. ³When all the people of Israel saw the fire come down and the glory of the LORD on the temple, they bowed down on the pavement with their faces to the ground, and worshiped and gave thanks to the LORD, saying,

> "For he is good,
>   for his steadfast love endures forever."

⁴Then the king and all the people offered sacrifice before the LORD.

Malachi 1:10–14

¹⁰Oh, that someone among you would shut the temple doors, so that you would not kindle fire on my altar in vain! I have no pleasure in you, says the LORD of hosts, and I will not accept an offering from your hands. ¹¹For from the rising of the sun to its setting my name is great among the nations, and in every place incense is offered to my name, and a pure offering; for my name is great among the nations, says the LORD of hosts. ¹²But you profane it when you say that the

Lord's table is polluted, and the food for it may be despised. [13]"What a weariness this is," you say, and you sniff at me, says the LORD of hosts. You bring what has been taken by violence or is lame or sick, and this you bring as your offering! Shall I accept that from your hand? says the LORD. [14]Cursed be the cheat who has a male in the flock and vows to give it, and yet sacrifices to the Lord what is blemished; for I am a great King, says the LORD of hosts, and my name is reverenced among the nations.

UNDERSTANDING

Continue seeking the meaning of these inspired texts as they reveal the sacrificial system of the ancient covenant and the will of God for his people.

Eucharistic Prayer I stirs memories of Old Testament sacrifices: "Be pleased to look upon these offerings with a serene and kindly countenance, and to accept them, as once you were pleased to accept the gifts of your servant Abel the just, the sacrifice of Abraham, our father in faith, and the offering of your high priest Melchizedek, a holy sacrifice, a spotless victim." These sacrifices were acceptable to God because the gifts offered reflected the holiness and obedience of the persons offering them. This ancient sacrificial system, which occupies so much of the focus of the Old Testament, foreshadows the eucharistic sacrifice of the New Testament.

Under the covenant with Moses, God commanded his people to construct the tabernacle in the wilderness, an earthly representation of his heavenly throne room, and to offer acceptable sacrifices through the ministry of worthy priests. When Israel became a kingdom under David and Solomon, God commanded that the temple built in Jerusalem would be the only place where Israel might offer sacrifices acceptable to God. In Solomon's prayer of dedication, he offered petitions for the blessings that would come when God received the sacrifices and heard the prayers of the people that accompanied them. When Solomon finished the prayer, "fire came down from heaven" upon the altar of sacrifice and "the glory of the LORD filled the temple" (2 Chron 7:1). With the fire, a manifestation of God's glory, God indicated that he was accepting the sacrifices and taking them to himself. Spatial images fail to express the divine reality taking place: God's glory comes down from heaven; earthly gifts are brought up to God. In other words, heaven and earth are brought into a new relationship with each other, so that earthly things become holy, lifegiving, accepted by God and made his own.

When Jesus died on the cross and was laid in the tomb, God's glory came upon his body on the third day. His glorified body manifested the fact that God received and accepted the sacrifice he offered. The fire that came down upon Solomon's offerings offers us an image, a foreshadowing of the spiritual fire that comes down during the

Eucharistic Prayer to receive our offering. When the church presents bread and wine to God on the altar, the fire of the Holy Spirit comes upon our offering and the glory of God fills it so that it becomes a truly acceptable sacrifice. It becomes the glorified body and blood of Jesus Christ, the Lamb who was sacrificed to redeem humanity for God.

During Eucharistic Prayer I, the priest bows and prays: "In humble prayer we ask you, almighty God: command that these gifts be borne by the hands of your holy Angel to your altar on high in the sight of your divine majesty, so that all of us who through this participation at the altar receive the most holy Body and Blood of your Son, may be filled with every grace and heavenly blessing." The liturgies of heaven and earth are united as God receives our offering and fills us with all the grace and blessings of Christ's eternal sacrifice. During Eucharistic Prayer II, the priest holds his hands over the offerings and prays: "Make holy, therefore, these gifts, we pray, by sending down your Spirit upon them like the dewfall, so that they may become for us the Body and Blood of our Lord, Jesus Christ." From the ancient sacrifices to the eternal sacrifice of Christ, it is always God who sanctifies acceptable sacrifices made in his name. The sacrifice of the church is accepted by God because the Father sees and loves in us what he sees and loves in Christ.

In the prophecy of Malachi, God expresses his displeasure at the sacrifices of the people of Israel and refuses to accept their offering (Mal 1:10). Their sacrifices are flawed and their heart is not in their offering. Instead, God would receive "a pure offering" from all the other nations of the world, "from the rising of the sun to its setting" (Mal 1:11). The early Christians understood this prophecy of Malachi to refer to the Eucharist. The Didache, written about AD 100, identifies the "pure offering" of Malachi with the Eucharist (*Didache* 14). Justin Martyr, in about AD 155, says that in Malachi, God "speaks of those Gentiles, namely us [Christians] who in every place offer sacrifices to him, that is, the bread of the Eucharist and also the cup of the Eucharist" (*Dialogue with Trypho*, 41). Irenaeus, too, in about AD 190, spoke about Malachi's prophecy: "By these words he makes it plain that the former people will cease to make offerings to God; but that in every place sacrifice will be offered to him, and indeed, a pure one, for his name is glorified among the Gentiles" (*Against Heresies* 4:17:5).

Eucharistic Prayer III alludes to Malachi's prophecy and beautifully expresses the universal quality of Christ's sacrifice: "You never cease to gather a people to yourself, so that from the rising of the sun to its setting a pure sacrifice may be offered to your name." In this sacrificial worship we are united with those celebrating the same sacrament in every place throughout the world.

While the doctrine of the Mass as sacrifice has been subject to mischaracterization and exaggeration, nonetheless, the church throughout its history, from the East to the

West, has taught the sacrificial character of the church's offering. The sacrifice offered in the Eucharist is not a new and separate sacrifice from Christ's one sacrifice on the cross. Rather, the re-presentation of the sacrifice is a mysterious participation in his one and only sacrifice for the world.

REFLECTING

Spend some time reflecting on the implications of these biblical and liturgical texts and consider what they can tell us about the eucharistic sacrifice of Christ.

- The Mass is the re-presentation of the sacrifice of Christ, an offering that is quite different from the sacrifices under the old covenant. What are some of the major differences between the sacrifices in the temple and the Mass?

- Eucharistic Prayer III expresses the universality of Christ's sacrifice: "from the rising of the sun to its setting a pure sacrifice may be offered to your name." In what ways does offering the eucharistic sacrifice unite us to God and to one another, vertically and horizontally?

- The prayer that beseeches the Father to send forth the Holy Spirit to transform the gifts into the body and blood of his Son is called the Epiclesis. Here is the invocation of Eucharistic Prayer III: "Therefore, O Lord, we pray: may this same Holy Spirit graciously sanctify these offerings, that they may become the Body and Blood of our Lord Jesus Christ for the celebration of this great mystery, which he himself left us as an eternal covenant." The Eucharist is an action of the Trinity. What is the role of the three persons of the Trinity in the Eucharistic Prayer?

PRAYING

Lift up your heart to the Lord and respond in prayer to the great gift of the Eucharist.

- Lord God of hosts, from the rising of the sun to its setting, your name is proclaimed among the nations through the pure offering of Jesus, your Soou send forth the fire of your Holy Spirit upon the eucharistic gifts, enkindle your whole church with the fire of your love.

Continue in silent prayer as you reflect on the great mystery of Christ's sacramental presence on the altar.

ACTING

Try to integrate the prayer of the Eucharist into the situations of your daily life.

- In the intercessory prayer of Eucharistic Prayer III, we pray: "Be pleased to confirm in faith and charity your pilgrim Church on earth." In what sense do I consider myself a pilgrim on the way? What can I do remind myself that I am a pilgrim seeking my true home?

Eucharistic Prayer: The part of the Mass that includes the consecration of the bread & wine. It begins with the preface & concludes with the great Amen.

Longest prayer of the mass. Has several different parts (8):
Preface
Acclamation
Epiclesis
Consecration
Anamnesis
Oblation
Intercessions
Doxology

LESSON 24

Christ's One Sacrifice Offered for All

LISTENING

Christ has offered us the new and living way to experience forgiveness and union with God. Listen carefully as the inspired writer speaks of Christ's fulfillment of Israel's recurring sacrifices.

Hebrews 10:1–25

¹Since the law has only a shadow of the good things to come and not the true form of these realities, it can never, by the same sacrifices that are continually offered year after year, make perfect those who approach. ²Otherwise, would they not have ceased being offered, since the worshipers, cleansed once for all, would no longer have any consciousness of sin? ³But in these sacrifices there is a reminder of sin year after year. ⁴For it is impossible for the blood of bulls and goats to take away sins. ⁵Consequently, when Christ came into the world, he said,

> "Sacrifices and offerings you have not desired,
>   but a body you have prepared for me;
> ⁶in burnt offerings and sin offerings
>   you have taken no pleasure.
> ⁷Then I said, 'See, God, I have come to do your will, O God'
>   (in the scroll of the book it is written of me)."

⁸When he said above, "You have neither desired nor taken pleasure in sacrifices and offerings and burnt offerings and sin offerings" (these are offered according to the law), ⁹then he added, "See, I have come to do your will." He abolishes the first in order to establish the second. ¹⁰And it is by God's will that we have been sanctified through the offering of the body of Jesus Christ once for all.

¹¹And every priest stands day after day at his service, offering again and again the same sacrifices that can never take away sins. ¹²But when Christ had offered for all time a single sacrifice for sins, "he sat down at the right hand of God," ¹³and since then has been waiting "until his enemies would be made a footstool for his feet." ¹⁴For by a single offering he has perfected for all time those who are sanctified. ¹⁵And the Holy Spirit also testifies to us, for after saying,

¹⁶"This is the covenant that I will make with them
   after those days, says the Lord:
I will put my laws in their hearts,
   and I will write them on their minds,"

¹⁷he also adds,

"I will remember their sins and their lawless deeds no more."

¹⁸Where there is forgiveness of these, there is no longer any offering for sin.

¹⁹Therefore, my friends, since we have confidence to enter the sanctuary by the blood of Jesus, ²⁰by the new and living way that he opened for us through the curtain (that is, through his flesh), ²¹and since we have a great priest over the house of God, ²²let us approach with a true heart in full assurance of faith, with our hearts sprinkled clean from an evil conscience and our bodies washed with pure water. ²³Let us hold fast to the confession of our hope without wavering, for he who has promised is faithful. ²⁴And let us consider how to provoke one another to love and good deeds, ²⁵not neglecting to meet together, as is the habit of some, but encouraging one another, and all the more as you see the Day approaching.

UNDERSTANDING

After your reflective reading of the Scripture, continue to search for its meaning and significance in God's plan for the church.

The letter to the Hebrews demonstrates how the worship of God under the old law has been replaced by the new worship in Christ. This passage uses numerous liturgical terms that have been transferred from the ancient temple to the new, eternal offering of Christ: sacrifice, worshipers, the scroll of the book, offerings, priesthood, the body of Jesus, the blood of Jesus, sanctification, covenant, sanctuary, the assembly of believers, and the approaching Day of the Lord. These verses express the summit of salvation history — the perpetual sacrifice of Christ — the reality that the church celebrates in every eucharistic liturgy.

The sacrifices of the old covenant were a "shadow" of the good things to come in Christ, not a "true form" of these realities (v. 1). The Israelites had an indirect relationship to Christ through the shadow; we, however, have a direct relationship through the true form of Christ that has now been revealed. The ancient sacrifices were incomplete and repetitious, but they prefigured the once-for-all, perfectly complete sacrifice of Christ.

The sacrifices of the Mosaic law brought a ritual and superficial cleansing of sin, but they were never able to bring about the kind of forgiveness that would bring people inner peace. They were unable to inwardly release the human conscience from guilt. In fact, these sacrifices were repeated reminders of sin and continually emphasized human guilt and unworthiness before God (vv. 2–4).

The new covenant offers us a way to be sanctified, to receive true and lasting forgiveness of sins: "through the offering of the body of Jesus" (v. 10) and "by the blood of Jesus" (v. 19). The author places the words of Psalm 40 on the lips of Jesus (v. 5–9). The obedient will of Jesus, who offered his body and shed his blood, replaces the numerous sacrifices of old. Because of who Jesus is and the nature of his self-offering, he bestows upon us complete and interior forgiveness, absolving our consciences from guilt.

Just as the many sacrifices under the law have been replaced by the one sacrifice of Christ, the many priests have been replaced by the one priest (vv. 11–14). Christ, who "offered for all time a single sacrifice for sins," has been raised from death and exalted to God's right hand, where he continually offers priestly intercession and mediates on our behalf. While he waits for his enemies to be made his footstool — injustice, hatred, despair, loneliness, sickness, and death — we are being perfected and sanctified.

Finally, the author urges the Christian faithful to assemble together for worship (v. 25). This Christian assembly is the ideal setting for mutual encouragement and exhorting one another to love and good deeds. Through the church's eucharistic worship, the one perpetual sacrifice of Christ is re-presented on altars throughout the world until he comes again. The memorial of his ageless sacrifice transcends space and time, making us participants in Christ's offering at the throne of the Father. The body and blood of Jesus, offered for our sanctification and received in Eucharist, perfects us and invites us to experience God's merciful forgiveness.

REFLECTING

Bringing God's word into the present context of your life, spend some time reflecting on these questions.

- The author of the letter to the Hebrews discusses the sacrifices, offerings, burnt-offerings, and sin-offerings of the ancient Torah. In what sense were these many sacrifices a "shadow" of the good things to come, offering the Israelites an indirect relationship to Christ through the shadow?

- Since Christ is the "great priest over the house of God," the author of Hebrews urges the community to "approach" with a heart full of faith, hope, and love (vv.21–24). In what way does each of these three virtues help me prepare for and live out the holy sacrifice of the Mass?

- "The Mystery of Faith," proclaimed in every Eucharistic Prayer, is a succinct expression of our incorporation into the paschal mystery. Each of the three options is a biblical acclamation addressed to Christ: "We proclaim your Death, O Lord, and profess your Resurrection until you come again" (1 Cor 11:26); "When we eat this Bread and drink this Cup, we proclaim your Death, O Lord, until you come again" (1 Cor 11:26); "Save us, Savior of the world (John 4:42), for by your Cross and Resurrection you have set us free." From these three acclamations, how do I describe the essence of the mystery of faith?

Praying

Give praise to God who has given you forgiveness and life through the sacrifice of Jesus Christ.

- All glory and honor is yours, Almighty Father, for giving us the bread of life and the cup of our salvation. May we proclaim the death and resurrection of your Son, Jesus Christ, in the unity of the Holy Spirit, until he comes again.

Continue speaking to God, asking for the gifts of faith, hope, and love.

Acting

The three acclamations of the people — the Sanctus, the Mystery of Faith, and the final Amen — convince us that the Eucharistic Prayer, while proclaimed by the priest, is nevertheless the prayer of the entire assembly or, better still, the prayer of Christ and his people.

- Concluding the final doxology — "Through him, with him, and in him" — the Amen places the seal of the assembly's approval on all that has been said and done in the Eucharistic Prayer (Rom 11:36; Rev 1:6). What do you wish to ponder or imagine as you sing or say Amen? Why should the assembly try to make this Amen be a heartfelt and passionate acclamation?

Group Session Guide for Section V

Begin with hospitality and welcome. Offer any announcements or instructions before entering the spirit of focused discussion. Discuss these questions or those of your own choosing:

1. In what sense is the Liturgy of the Eucharist the culmination of salvation history right before your eyes?

2. How can developing a eucharistic spirituality help you participate more fully in the Mass and live out its reality more consciously in your life?

3. What is the symbolic significance of the gifts of bread and wine as an expression of your own participation in the Mass? (Lesson 19)

4. How does the uniting of your imperfect works with the sacrifice of Christ in the Mass help you understand how the good efforts of your life have a role in your salvation? (Lesson 19)

5. In what ways might an experience of God's awesome majesty and transcendent holiness, as sung in the Sanctus, lead to internal change within a person like Isaiah? (Lesson 20)

6. As you live out the invitation, "Lift up your heart," how does this practice give you hope and confidence when you unite your life throughout the week with your Sunday Mass? (Lesson 20)

7. Jesus prayed that his church be one, and in our Eucharist we pray for the unity of the church throughout the world. Though unity is the work of the Holy Spirit, what is your role in living out the church's sacrament of unity? (Lesson 21)

8. In what ways do the words and gestures of the Institution Narrative of the Mass express the heart of the Eucharist? (Lesson 22)

9. The Institution Narrative states that the blood of the covenant is poured out "for you and for many." In what way does this express both the inclusiveness of God's gift of salvation and the necessity of human acceptance of the gift? (Lesson 22)

10. "You never cease to gather a people to yourself, so that from the rising of the sun to its setting a pure sacrifice may be offered to your name" (Eucharistic Prayer III). How do these words express to you the full meaning of Malachi's prophecy and the universal quality of Christ's sacrifice? (Lesson 23)

11. Choose one of the acclamations of the Mystery of Faith. In what ways does this acclamation express your incorporation into the paschal mystery of Christ? (Lesson 24)

12. What are some of the words of the Eucharistic Prayer that have new meaning for you as a result of this study?

Remind group members to complete the six lessons from section VI during the week ahead.

Offer prayers of thanksgiving aloud to God for the insights and understanding you gained in the lesson this week.

Offer prayers for your own needs and the needs of others. Pray for the grace to act upon any decisions or resolutions you have made during your study.

Conclude together: *Our Father, who art in heaven ...*

Section VI

The Communion Rite and Dismissal

The Eucharist is not only a sacrifice, but also a banquet. It is only when it retains these two aspects that the Mass fully expresses the nature of the Christ's gift and of Christian life. Christ not only gave himself up to death for our redemption, but he rose to give us the fullness of life. Life as his disciple is not only self-giving and sacrifice, but also joy and community. These aspects of Eucharist are inseparable: the sacrificial memorial in which the sacrifice of the cross is perpetuated and the sacred banquet of communion with the Lord's body and blood.

We have seen how ancient covenants were established by means of a sacrifice followed by a sacred banquet. These covenants foreshadow the new and everlasting covenant established by Jesus. This permanent bond with God is renewed whenever the church celebrates the Mass, and its saving effects are made available for all who faithfully participate in the eucharistic sacrifice and banquet. In this way, Jesus has made us a eucharistic people from the very origins of the church.

The Mass' sacrificial character as a memorial of the cross is expressed primarily in the Eucharistic Prayer. By making his body and blood present under separate appearances, Jesus wished to signify the violent death he accepted and offered to his Father out of love for the world. The Eucharistic Prayer sacramentally makes present the sacrifice that it signifies. The sacrifice of Christ on the cross and the sacrifice of the Eucharist are one single sacrifice. In the Mystery of Faith we proclaim with Paul: "As often as you eat this bread and drink this cup, you proclaim the Lord's death until he comes" (1 Cor 11:26).

In addition to memorializing Christ's death, the eucharistic celebration also commemorates his resurrection and ascension to the Father — the complete paschal mystery. Jesus becomes present to us as the glorious victor over sin and death. He continues to make present in the Mass the redemption and salvation given by his unique sacrifice until he comes again. For this reason, the Eucharist is also a sacred banquet of his own body and blood. The spiritual nourishment of Communion empowers us to live ever more completely in the likeness of the Son, in his obedience, fidelity, and love for the Father. In this holy banquet, we draw the strength to make our lives a complete gift to God and we are fed with the food of everlasting life.

The Mass looks backward as a memorial of Christ's sacrifice, forward as a foretaste of the heavenly banquet, and to the present moment as the eucharistic

Christ is incarnate in the lives of individual believers and within the assembly of his church. The Rite of Communion are the prayers and rituals that surround this intimate encounter when we receive the living Christ in a true, real, and substantial manner: body, blood, soul, and divinity. The Lord's Prayer asks for the deliverance from evil and the coming of God's kingdom. The Rite of Peace expresses the unity and reconciliation of believers in preparation for Communion. The Fraction of the eucharistic bread signifies that the many faithful are made one body as they are invited to the banquet of Christ. After Communion, the Concluding Rites focus on the sending forth of the community so that those who are nourished and transformed in the sacrament may in turn become sacraments to the world.

- Why are the elements of sacrifice and banquet two inseparable aspects of the Mass?

- Why does Jesus give himself to his church through the nourishment of a banquet?

- In what sense is the Concluding Rite the natural response to receiving Communion?

LESSON 25

Awaiting the Blessed Hope, We Pray as Jesus Taught Us

Listening

Jesus taught us to pray to the Father, so with expectant faith we dare to say the words he gave to us. Let the prayer of Jesus from the gospel become your prayer this day.

Matthew 6:7–15

7"When you are praying, do not heap up empty phrases as the Gentiles do; for they think that they will be heard because of their many words. 8Do not be like them, for your Father knows what you need before you ask him.

9"Pray then in this way:
Our Father in heaven,
  hallowed be your name.
  10Your kingdom come.
  Your will be done,
    on earth as it is in heaven.
  11Give us this day our daily bread.
  12And forgive us our debts,
    as we also have forgiven our debtors.
  13And do not bring us to the time of trial,
    but rescue us from the evil one.

14For if you forgive others their trespasses, your heavenly Father will also forgive you; 15but if you do not forgive others, neither will your Father forgive your trespasses.

1 Chronicles 29:10–13

[10]Then David blessed the LORD in the presence of all the assembly; David said: "Blessed are you, O LORD, the God of our ancestor Israel, forever and ever. [11]Yours, O LORD, are the greatness, the power, the glory, the victory, and the majesty; for all that is in the heavens and on the earth is yours; yours is the kingdom, O LORD, and you are exalted as head above all. [12]Riches and honor come from you, and you rule over all. In your hand are power and might; and it is in your hand to make great and to give strength to all. [13]And now, our God, we give thanks to you and praise your glorious name.

UNDERSTANDING

Try to understand why the Lord's Prayer is the ideal prayer in preparation for receiving Communion and explore its full meaning through the ongoing tradition of the church.

The Communion Rite begins with the Lord's Prayer, the prayer that Jesus taught his disciples when they asked him how to pray. It has been called the prayer *par excellence* because when we pray it with Jesus, our voices blend with his and our hearts open to our Father in heaven. When Jesus taught his disciples to pray, he did much more than give them a simple prayer to memorize and repeat. Jesus showed them how to address God with intimacy and trust. Because it addresses God as "our Father" and not "my Father," it is a prayer that is always prayed in union with the church. For this reason, it was included in the church's eucharistic liturgy in the apostolic period and has long been a prominent part of the Mass.

Like the Eucharist, the Lord's Prayer focuses on the present with an eye to the future. It exhorts us to pray for the coming of God's kingdom as we celebrate the Lord's presence in our midst (Matt 6:10). When prayed in eucharistic worship, the prayer expresses our longing for that time in which there will be no more sadness and pain, when sin and death have vanished, when salvation will be manifested in every corner of the globe and in every corner of our hearts. We pray with Jesus for the full realization, "on earth as it is in heaven," of that prayer he offered to the Father in Gethsemane immediately after the Last Supper: "your will be done."

One of the ways the early Christians referred to the Eucharist was "our *epiousios* bread," which we usually translate in the Lord's Prayer as "our daily bread." However, the exact meaning of the Greek adjective is uncertain because it is found nowhere else in the ancient Greek language. Literally it means "super-essential," and it was translated by St. Jerome as "supersubstantial." Many biblical commentators suggest that the early Christians coined this new word to refer to their new experience of Eucharist, a unique meal like no other in which the risen Lord was present to his followers. Though the kingdom is coming in the future, we have a foretaste of that banquet today in "our bread," "our meal," the bread of life.

Following the Lord's Prayer, the priest expands upon the last petition and asks for deliverance from the powers of evil in a prayer known as the embolism (interpolation). He elaborates on the many implications of the Lord's Prayer and asks God for peace, freedom from sin, and safety from distress for the entire community, and he concludes with a phrase similar to what Paul wrote to Titus: "as we await the blessed hope and the coming of our Savior, Jesus Christ" (Titus 2:13).

The embolism is followed by a doxology that is prayed by the assembly: "For the kingdom, the power and the glory are yours now and forever." Adding a doxology to the end of prayers goes back to the Old Testament, as we see, for example, in the concluding verses of Psalm 72. That practice was continued in the church, as, for example, a trinitarian doxology, "Glory be to the Father, and to the Son, and to the Holy Spirit…," was added to the end of the psalms when prayed in the Liturgy of the Hours.

The prayer of David from 1 Chronicles is an example of the kind of praise found in the biblical doxologies. In fact, the doxology attributes to God "the kingdom," "the power," and "the glory" (1 Chron 29:11). While David attributed these qualities to God "forever and ever" (1 Chron 29:10), the liturgy of the church proclaims them "now and forever," emphasizing the reality that God is present in the Mass with his kingdom, power, and glory in the living presence of Jesus Christ. What we experience under sacramental signs now in the Eucharist will be fully revealed when we experience the blessed hope, the glorious coming of our Savior.

The doxology of the liturgy was added to the prayer of Jesus by the early church. The community drew on its Jewish heritage and ended the Lord's Prayer with the doxology, as we see in the ancient text of the *Didache*. Since this became a customary way of concluding the Lord's Prayer, some scribes added this ending to their copies of the prayer in Matthew's gospel. Though the oldest manuscripts of the gospel do not include the doxology, it is certainly an ancient Christian prayer and one that belongs in the church's liturgy.

REFLECTION

Consider the fuller meaning and significance of the Lord's Prayer in the context of the church's eucharistic liturgy.

- God gave a portion of daily manna to his people in the wilderness (Exod 16:4), and throughout the Bible, God's gift of bread becomes a sign of his care and salvation (Ps 78:24–25). Whenever Jesus gives bread to his people in the gospels, those passages are laden with eucharistic overtones. What are some of those passages and what do they tell me about Eucharist, the bread of life?

- In the context of the church's liturgy, the petitions of the Lord's Prayer take on a fuller meaning. We could even say that the Mass fulfills the Lord's Prayer word for word. Give some examples from the Lord's Prayer that are fulfilled or completed in the celebration of the Mass.

- To introduce the Lord's Prayer, the priest says, "At the Savior's command and formed by divine teaching, we dare to say." Why has the church resisted appending the doxology directly on the end of the Lord's Prayer during the liturgy?

PRAYING

Let the Bible and the liturgy continue to enrich the vocabulary and style of your prayer.

- Our Father, hallowed be your name. May we long for the coming of your kingdom as we celebrate the presence of your Son among us. Forgive us our sins as we forgive one another. Give us today the bread that sustains us forever.

Continue to form the words of your prayer as it flows from your heart.

ACTING

Continue letting the words you pray become the life you live.

- Pray again the words of the Lord's Prayer. Choose one of the petitions to focus on and live throughout your day.

Offering the Sign of Peace to One Another

LISTENING

Allow the inspired word of God to teach you and transform you as you read.

Matthew 5:21–24

²¹"You have heard that it was said to those of ancient times, 'You shall not murder'; and 'whoever murders shall be liable to judgment.' ²²But I say to you that if you are angry with a brother or sister, you will be liable to judgment; and if you insult a brother or sister, you will be liable to the council; and if you say, 'You fool,' you will be liable to the hell of fire. ²³So when you are offering your gift at the altar, if you remember that your brother or sister has something against you, ²⁴leave your gift there before the altar and go; first be reconciled to your brother or sister, and then come and offer your gift.

John 14:25–29

²⁵"I have said these things to you while I am still with you. ²⁶But the Advocate, the Holy Spirit, whom the Father will send in my name, will teach you everything, and remind you of all that I have said to you. ²⁷Peace I leave with you; my peace I give to you. I do not give to you as the world gives. Do not let your hearts be troubled, and do not let them be afraid. ²⁸You heard me say to you, 'I am going away, and I am coming to you.' If you loved me, you would rejoice that I am going to the Father, because the Father is greater than I. ²⁹And now I have told you this before it occurs, so that when it does occur, you may believe.

Romans 16:12–16

¹²Greet those workers in the Lord, Tryphaena and Tryphosa. Greet the beloved Persis, who has worked hard in the Lord. ¹³Greet Rufus, chosen in the Lord; and

greet his mother — a mother to me also. [14]Greet Asyncritus, Phlegon, Hermes, Patrobas, Hermas, and the brothers and sisters who are with them. [15]Greet Philologus, Julia, Nereus and his sister, and Olympas, and all the saints who are with them. [16]Greet one another with a holy kiss. All the churches of Christ greet you.

UNDERSTANDING

Seek to understand the meaning of the ancient kiss of peace and why it is such an integral part of the church's liturgy.

The letters of Paul are full of personal greetings. He believed that all believers are joined in the body of Christ, and he expected that union to be expressed in the way they relate to one another. At the end of several of his letters, he urged believers to "greet one another with a holy kiss" (Rom 16:16; 1 Cor 16:20; 2 Cor 13:12; 1 Thes 5:26).

In the Old Testament, a kiss on the cheek expressed the emotional embracing of family or the heartfelt affection of close friends. It could indicate the intimacy of reconciliation, as when Jacob and Esau were reunited (Gen 33:4). The kiss could also indicate intimacy restored, as when Joseph and his brothers met together again (Gen 45:15). In the New Testament, the kiss remained a sign of affection and cherished relationship, as when the Father greeted his prodigal son (Luke 15:20) or when Paul parted from the Ephesian elders (Acts 20:38). Jesus rebuked Simon for not greeting him with a kiss because it was taken for granted that persons close to one another would exchange a kiss upon meeting (Luke 7:45). The kiss was such an important sign of genuine affection, that the deceitful kiss of Judas used to identify Jesus at his arrest (Matt 26:49) was seen by the early church as the worst kind of betrayal.

The "holy kiss" that Paul urged the members of the churches to exchange seems to be a symbolic and ritualized action. Of course, for any ritual practice to be authentic it must interiorly convey what it outwardly expresses. The "holy kiss" was no less affectionate and genuine because it was a symbolic action. It expressed Christian fellowship and *agape* (self-giving love), as seen in the closing of Peter's letter: "Greet one another with a kiss of love" (1 Pet 5:14). Baptized believers offered the kiss to one another primarily, though not exclusively, in the church's worship. On the Lord's Day the community gathered to hear the ancient Scriptures and the letters addressed to them by the apostles, then they exchanged the holy kiss after the readings and in preparation for eucharistic communion.

This ritual kiss later came to be called the "kiss of peace" or simply, "the peace." It was exchanged during eucharistic worship, not simply as a greeting, but as a sign of reconciliation and unity between the members of the church. The *Didache* insisted that members of the community be reconciled to one another before they could share the Eucharist. This practice is rooted in the teachings of Jesus: "When you are offering your gift at the altar, if you remember that your brother or sister has something against you, leave your gift there before the altar and go; first be reconciled to your brother or sister, and then come and offer your gift" (Matt 5:23–24). Justin Martyr, writing in about AD 155, mentions the exchange of the kiss within the Eucharist (*First Apology*). At the end of the second century, Tertullian considered the sign of peace the ratification of the church's prayer, calling it the "seal of prayer." He asked, "What prayer is complete if divorced from the holy kiss?" Through the centuries, the kiss of peace took different forms within the Mass, but essentially it expressed the peace and unity that Christ left to his church and that he continues to communicate through the Holy Spirit (John 14:27).

In today's Rite of Peace, the church asks for peace and unity for herself and the whole human family as a preparation for Communion. The manner of offering one another the sign of peace is established according to the customs and the culture of the people in each region of the world. It must be a reverent expression of Christian unity and a genuine offer of the peace of Christ to one another.

REFLECTING

Allow the Scriptures and liturgical actions to interact with your own world of ideas, concerns, thoughts, and feelings.

- Jesus said, "First be reconciled to your brother or sister, and then come and offer your gift." Why would it be important to be at peace with our brothers and sisters before offering our lives with Christ's sacrifice and receiving him in Communion?

- In the Rite of Peace, we plead with the Lord, "Look not on our sins, but on the faith of your Church, and graciously grant her peace and unity in accordance with your will. Who live and reign for ever and ever." While the ritual can often become a boisterous moment of greeting others, we need to remember that it primarily expresses our unity in Christ and our desire to experience his peace and communion together. How can I be more aware of the rite's primary meaning?

- Though in many Eastern rites of the liturgy, the sign of peace is placed at the beginning of the Liturgy of the Eucharist, the Roman rite continues to place it before Communion. What might be some reasons why the Rite of Peace is appropriately employed as an immediate preparation for Communion?

Praying

Pray as part of the reconciled community that Christ has formed in his church.

- Lord Jesus, in the Eucharist you share the gift of unity and peace with Jews and Gentiles, slaves and free people, women and men, rich and poor. When I share your peace, I am united even to those with whom I feel no natural bond. Open my heart to all those who share Eucharist with me.

In wordless silence, hand over to God those aspects of your life over which you have no control. Trust that God will give you the gift of love and peace.

ACTING

Consider how the peace ritual can have a more lasting impact on your daily life.

- In addressing his apostles at the Last Supper, Jesus said, "Peace I leave with you; my peace I give to you. I do not give to you as the world gives. Do not let your hearts be troubled, and do not let them be afraid" (John 14:27). What is the difference between the peace the world attempts to offer and the peace that only Jesus can give? How can I open my life more fully to receive this gift?

LESSON 27

Lamb of God Who Takes Away the Sin of the World

LISTENING

Ask the Holy Spirit to guide your listening to this text as God's Spirit led John the Evangelist and John the Seer to write them. Let these words lead you to adore Christ, the paschal lamb.

John 1:29–37

[29]The next day [John the Baptist] saw Jesus coming toward him and declared, "Here is the Lamb of God who takes away the sin of the world! [30]This is he of whom I said, 'After me comes a man who ranks ahead of me because he was before me.' [31]I myself did not know him; but I came baptizing with water for this reason, that he might be revealed to Israel." [32]And John testified, "I saw the Spirit descending from heaven like a dove, and it remained on him. [33]I myself did not know him, but the one who sent me to baptize with water said to me, 'He on whom you see the Spirit descend and remain is the one who baptizes with the Holy Spirit.' [34]And I myself have seen and have testified that this is the Son of God."

[35]The next day John again was standing with two of his disciples, [36]and as he watched Jesus walk by, he exclaimed, "Look, here is the Lamb of God!" [37]The two disciples heard him say this, and they followed Jesus.

Revelation 19:4–9

[4]And the twenty-four elders and the four living creatures fell down and worshiped God who is seated on the throne, saying,

"Amen. Hallelujah!"

⁵And from the throne came a voice saying,

> "Praise our God,
>> all you his servants,
> and all who fear him,
>> small and great."

⁶Then I heard what seemed to be the voice of a great multitude, like the sound of many waters and like the sound of mighty thunderpeals, crying out,

> "Hallelujah!
> For the Lord our God
>> the Almighty reigns.
> ⁷Let us rejoice and exult
>> and give him the glory,
> for the marriage of the Lamb has come,
>> and his bride has made herself ready;
> ⁸to her it has been granted to be clothed
>> with fine linen, bright and pure" —

for the fine linen is the righteous deeds of the saints.

⁹And the angel said to me, "Write this: Blessed are those who are invited to the marriage supper of the Lamb." And he said to me, "These are true words of God."

UNDERSTANDING

Continue exploring the significance of these passages for our worship of Christ as the Lamb of God.

These biblical texts lead us to understand the tradition handed on to the church by the apostles — that Christ is "our paschal lamb" (1 Cor 5:7) who was sacrificed for our salvation and whose flesh and blood we eat and drink in remembrance of his saving death and resurrection. The origin of the title reaches back to Abraham who, when his son Isaac was carrying the wood for his own sacrifice on his back, assured him, "God himself will provide the lamb" (Gen 22:8). To commemorate God's liberation of the Hebrews from Egypt, God instituted the Passover feast, in which every family was to take a pure, unblemished lamb to sacrifice, mark their homes with its blood, then eat its roasted flesh in a ritual meal of remembrance.

When John the Baptist cried out "Here is the Lamb of God who takes away the sin of the world!" (John 1:29, 36), the fulfillment of God's ancient promise to provide the lamb was made known. The gospel of John then develops the reality of Jesus as the

Passover sacrifice and meal. As Jesus is handed over to death, the gospel declares that it was the day of preparation for the Passover at about noon (John 19:14), the very hour when the sacrifice of the Passover lambs began in Jerusalem. The true Lamb of God would be sacrificed at the very moment the Passover lambs were sacrificed in the temple. In this way, John unites the sacrifice of Jesus with the Eucharist of his church. Christ's glorious death and resurrection is the Passover of our liberation, the paschal mystery re-presented and memorialized in every Mass.

Every time we chant, "Lamb of God, you take away the sins of the world," we are speaking in the present tense. Christ's work of redemption did not conclude with his death, but is continual and ongoing. The Lamb of God continues to make intercession to the Father. The sacrifice of Christ and the Eucharist are one, and at the Mass the church is present at this single redemptive event. Christ's perpetual sacrifice is forever valid and conferring salvation. Every Mass is offered for the expiation of our sins.

In the book of Revelation, "the Lamb" is the principal image of Christ. The visionary sees the Lamb, slain in sacrifice though standing in God's presence. The vision is an expression of the timeless sacrifice of Jesus being offered eternally to the Father. All of creation participates in this cosmic worship of God in the heavenly liturgy. Whenever we celebrate the Eucharist on earth, we become part of the everlasting offering of Christ that John describes in his vision.

The book of Revelation, and indeed the entire Bible, leads up to the proclamation of the marriage of the Lamb and his bride (Rev 19:7). This is an image of the perfect union of Christ and his church in a love that is fruitful and eternal. This is the final goal of salvation history, the fullness of blessing that God has desired to bestow on all people. This is the saving history that continues and reaches its climactic fulfillment in every Mass. In the Eucharist we receive a taste of what we will experience for all eternity, when we join with the heavenly throng in the wedding feast with Christ: "Blessed are those who are invited to the marriage supper of the Lamb" (Rev 19:9). In receiving Communion we anticipate the final coming of Christ, when all sin and death will be no more, at the table of the Lamb in the heavenly kingdom

Immediately before Communion, the priest genuflects and presents the consecrated host to the people, proclaiming first the words of John the Baptist (John 1:29): "Behold the Lamb of God, behold him who takes away the sins of the world." He follows these words with words of the angel to John the visionary (Rev 19:9): "Blessed are those called to the supper of the Lamb." Like John who fell down to worship at the words of the angel, we kneel and proclaim our unworthiness: "*Domine, non sum dingus* — Lord, I am not worthy."

REFLECTING

Reflect on the implications of these biblical texts for the liturgy of the church and our salvation from sin.

- Paul the apostle proclaimed, "Our paschal lamb, Christ, has been sacrificed. Therefore, let us celebrate the festival." He spoke in his own day about the new Passover in Christ, celebrated in the church's Eucharist. In what ways do the Scriptures connect the church's eucharistic festival with the sacrifice of the Lamb?

- When Jesus told the centurion that he would come and heal his son, the centurion replied, "Lord, I am not worthy to have you come under my roof; but only speak the word, and my servant will be healed" (Matt 8:8). Immediately before Christ comes to our home, our very bodies, in Communion, we make these words our own. How do these words of the gospel help form my heart as I prepare for Communion?

- After the centurion proclaimed his unworthiness and trust, Jesus praised the humble faith of the Gentile centurion and said, "Many will come from east and west and will eat with Abraham and Isaac and Jacob in the kingdom of heaven" (Matt 8:11). How does this allude to the prophecy of Malachi 1:11? What does the full context of the miracle account teach me about my response to the gift of the Eucharist?

PRAYING

Ask that the Holy Spirit, who guided your listening to God's word, will lead your response to that word in prayer.

- Lamb of God, you take away the sins of the world, have mercy on us. Thank you for calling me to share in your timeless sacrifice to the Father through the gift of the Eucharist. When I eat your sacred body and drink your precious blood, help me to live confidently and victoriously in you.

Rest with security in God's saving grace at work within your heart. Continue thanking Christ for his priceless gift.

ACTING

It is our responsibility to instill within ourselves the attitudes and virtues we proclaim in the liturgy.

- When we are invited to the supper of the Lamb in Communion, we reply, "Lord, I am not worthy that you should enter under my roof, but only say the word and my soul shall be healed." What can I do this week to cultivate a spirit of humility, faith, and gratitude in preparation for receiving Communion?

LESSON 28

Eating His Body and Drinking His Blood

LISTENING

Kiss the words of the gospel text and ask God to let these inspired words speak powerfully to you today. Read the words aloud so that you will experience them more fully by seeing them with your eyes, hearing them with your ears, and speaking them with your lips.

John 6:51–69

[51]"I am the living bread that came down from heaven. Whoever eats of this bread will live forever; and the bread that I will give for the life of the world is my flesh."

[52]The Jews then disputed among themselves, saying, "How can this man give us his flesh to eat?" [53]So Jesus said to them, "Very truly, I tell you, unless you eat the flesh of the Son of Man and drink his blood, you have no life in you. [54]Those who eat my flesh and drink my blood have eternal life, and I will raise them up on the last day; [55]for my flesh is true food and my blood is true drink. [56]Those who eat my flesh and drink my blood abide in me, and I in them. [57]Just as the living Father sent me, and I live because of the Father, so whoever eats me will live because of me. [58]This is the bread that came down from heaven, not like that which your ancestors ate, and they died. But the one who eats this bread will live forever." [59]He said these things while he was teaching in the synagogue at Capernaum.

[60]When many of his disciples heard it, they said, "This teaching is difficult; who can accept it?" [61]But Jesus, being aware that his disciples were complaining about it, said to them, "Does this offend you? [62]Then what if you were to see the Son of Man ascending to where he was before? [63]It is the spirit that gives life; the flesh is useless. The words that I have spoken to you are spirit and life. [64]But among you there are some who do not believe." For Jesus knew from the first who were the ones that did not believe, and who was the one that would betray him. [65]And

he said, "For this reason I have told you that no one can come to me unless it is granted by the Father."

⁶⁶Because of this many of his disciples turned back and no longer went about with him. ⁶⁷So Jesus asked the twelve, "Do you also wish to go away?" ⁶⁸Simon Peter answered him, "Lord, to whom can we go? You have the words of eternal life. ⁶⁹We have come to believe and know that you are the Holy One of God."

UNDERSTANDING

Seek to understand with your mind and heart the full implications of this gospel text for your faith in Christ's real presence in the Eucharist.

The entire gospel of John demonstrates how the eternal, life-giving Word of God "became flesh and lived among us" in the person of Jesus (1:14). This emphasis on the Incarnation carries over to John's emphasis on the real presence of Christ in the Eucharist. The eternal Word not only dwells with us but gives himself for us as our life-giving food: "The bread that I will give for the life of the world is my flesh" (v. 51). The word "give" here is a sacrificial term. Jesus is saying that he will "give" (that is, "offer") his "flesh" to God in sacrifice "for the life of the world." He is also saying, using a double meaning for the word "give," that he will give his flesh to be eaten by those who come to him. As in the thanksgiving offerings of the Torah, Jesus gives himself to God in sacrifice and he gives himself to eat in the sacrificial meal.

Jesus then emphasizes that eating his flesh and drinking his blood is the key to having "eternal life" (vv. 53–54). Eternal life in the gospel is true life that begins in the present and lasts forever. Jesus goes on to say that those who eat his flesh and drink his blood "abide" in him, and he in them (v. 56). To abide with him means to dwell or live with him. This reciprocal abiding, the disciples in Jesus and Jesus in the disciples, is a deep union or mutual indwelling. Jesus emphasizes that his flesh is "true food" and his blood is "true drink" (v. 55). Physically eating and drinking the sacramental flesh and blood of Christ in Eucharist joins believers to him in the most intimate way. Through the Eucharist, believers are invited to become one with Christ, as he and the Father are one, and through this intimate unity, to experience eternal life (v. 57).

The words of Jesus are deeply rooted in the Scriptures of Israel. He contrasts the bread their ancestors ate, the bread Moses provided in the wilderness, with the heavenly bread that Jesus provides, "the living bread that came down from heaven" (v. 51). Jesus also contrasts the Old Testament banquet, in which divine Wisdom offers the invitation to "eat of my bread and drink of the wine" (Prov 9:5) with the banquet of his own flesh and blood (vv. 54–56). When people taste of Wisdom, they hunger and thirst for more (Sir 24:21), but Jesus, the Wisdom of God incarnate, offers a food and drink that satisfies humanity's hunger and thirst completely.

This teaching of Jesus is described by his disciples as "difficult" to accept (v. 60), and many of them "turned back" and ceased following him (v. 66). Four times in rapid succession, Jesus has spoken of the necessity of eating his flesh and drinking his blood. These teachings of Jesus were so crucial that they demanded a personal decision. Yet, for that decision, human flesh is of no benefit (v. 63). Since the words of Jesus are "spirit and life," the disciples needed the gift of the Spirit to receive his words in faith. When Jesus asked the twelve if they wished to go away too, Simon Peter answered for them. Because they had come to trust that Jesus is "the Holy One of God," they were able to accept his eucharistic message as "the words of eternal life" (vv. 68–69).

John's emphasis on the Incarnation carried over to his emphasis on the real presence of Christ in the Eucharist. He is the Word made flesh that lived among us, is now glorified, and is present to us in sacrament. The Word of God made flesh has become Eucharist. The Eucharist is the sacramental climax of the mission of the Word of God to the world.

REFLECTING

Ponder these verses of John's gospel as you reflect on their challenge to your faith in the presence of Christ in Eucharist.

- This eucharistic discourse of Jesus focuses on the real and living presence of Jesus Christ in the church's Eucharist. Which of the verses most confirms my faith that Christ is truly present — body, blood, soul, and divinity — as I receive Communion?

- The real presence of Jesus Christ in the Eucharist means that he is objectively present to us, in contrast to something that is only mentally present to us, like an idea or memory. We may be low in faith, lacking in desire, or inattentive, but the risen Lord is truly there. What can deepen my faith in the real presence of Christ in the Eucharist?

- Following this eucharistic discourse of Jesus, many of his disciples departed from him and no longer followed him. Why is this teaching of Jesus so difficult to accept (v. 60)? Why have the church's beliefs about the real presence been so divisive for Christians in recent centuries?

PRAYING

Voice words of prayer in response to your hearing and pondering these words of Jesus.

- Lord Jesus, thank you for inviting me to share deeply in your life by eating your flesh as true food and drinking your blood as true drink. Deepen my awareness of your living presence as I receive Communion, and help me use every opportunity to draw closer to you.

The liturgy urges us to observe sacred silence after Communion. Spend a few moments in silence now, praying to God with gratitude in your heart.

ACTING

Consider how you might allow the grace of Christ's presence in the Eucharist to transform your life.

- The Word became flesh so that we might become participants in the divine nature. Following purification and illumination, the final stage of the spiritual life is deification, or participation in the life of God. How can worthy reception of Communion help me attain the goal of the spiritual life, continuing transformation in Christ?

The Many Become
the One Body of Christ

LISTENING

Paul explains to his readers what it means to partake of the Lord's table. Let his words speak to your heart and stir your will to wholehearted discipleship.

1 Corinthians 10:1–21

[1]I do not want you to be unaware, brothers and sisters, that our ancestors were all under the cloud, and all passed through the sea, [2]and all were baptized into Moses in the cloud and in the sea, [3]and all ate the same spiritual food, [4]and all drank the same spiritual drink. For they drank from the spiritual rock that followed them, and the rock was Christ. [5]Nevertheless, God was not pleased with most of them, and they were struck down in the wilderness.

[6]Now these things occurred as examples for us, so that we might not desire evil as they did. [7]Do not become idolaters as some of them did; as it is written, "The people sat down to eat and drink, and they rose up to play." [8]We must not indulge in sexual immorality as some of them did, and twenty-three thousand fell in a single day. [9]We must not put Christ to the test, as some of them did, and were destroyed by serpents. [10]And do not complain as some of them did, and were destroyed by the destroyer. [11]These things happened to them to serve as an example, and they were written down to instruct us, on whom the ends of the ages have come. [12]So if you think you are standing, watch out that you do not fall. [13]No testing has overtaken you that is not common to everyone. God is faithful, and he will not let you be tested beyond your strength, but with the testing he will also provide the way out so that you may be able to endure it.

[14]Therefore, my dear friends, flee from the worship of idols. [15]I speak as to sensible people; judge for yourselves what I say. [16]The cup of blessing that we bless, is it not a sharing in the blood of Christ? The bread that we break, is it not a sharing in the body of Christ? [17]Because there is one bread, we who are many are one body, for we all partake of the one bread. [18]Consider the people of Israel; are not those who eat the sacrifices partners in the altar? [19]What do I imply then? That food sacrificed to idols is anything, or that an idol is anything? [20]No, I imply that what pagans sacrifice, they sacrifice to demons and not to God. I do not want you to be partners with demons. [21]You cannot drink the cup of the Lord and the cup of demons. You cannot partake of the table of the Lord and the table of demons.

UNDERSTANDING

After your reflective reading of Paul's writing, continue exploring its implications for the church as it partakes in the one bread of Christ.

Paul's letters put us in contact with the apostolic church and show us that the Eucharist had a central place in the life of the early Christians. Since he intended his letters to be read in the liturgical assembly, he wrote them imagining himself personally addressing the eucharistic gathering. Because he frequently adapted greetings, prayers, blessings, and hymns from the Christian liturgy to include in his letters, they all express the flavor of the early celebrations of Eucharist. In writing this letter to the Corinthians, he provided the early church with important pastoral and theological terminology. He described the Eucharist as "spiritual food" and "spiritual drink" (v. 3), "the cup of blessing that we bless" and "the bread that we break," "sharing in the blood of Christ" and "sharing in the body of Christ" (v. 16), "the cup of the Lord," and "the table of the Lord" (v. 21).

Paul connects the story of the Exodus to the Christian sacraments of baptism and Eucharist. He demonstrates that "our ancestors" were all "baptized into Moses" by standing under the cloud and passing through the sea (vv. 1–2). This is a shadow of the spirit and water through which Christians are baptized into Christ. The ancestors also ate "spiritual food" and drank "spiritual drink" in the desert, foreshadowing the full reality to be later shared in the Christian Eucharist (vv. 3–4). Paul goes on to show that although the ancestors received great blessings from God, they still acted in ways that displeased God and they suffered the consequences of their unfaithful choices. Through these examples (v. 11), Paul teaches Christians not to assume God's favor because they have been given the marvelous spiritual nourishment of Christ's presence in the Eucharist. Rather, receiving Christ in the eucharistic assembly requires faithfulness to him and holiness of life.

Paul's teachings on the Eucharist in this section of his letter are not an elaborate doctrinal exposition but his response to an important question for believers living in the context of Greco-Roman culture: whether or not Christians could eat food that had been offered to idols. Paul explains his prohibition of this practice by referring to the true communion with Christ experienced by Christians in the Eucharist. The union experienced with Christ in Communion is real: the cup we bless is a "sharing in the blood of Christ"; the bread we break is a "sharing in the body of Christ" (v. 16). This communion with Christ also establishes a real unity with other believers who share the Eucharist. Those who partake of the "one bread" become "one body."

As God demanded the exclusive allegiance of his people in the desert when he gave them spiritual food and drink, so God demands even greater fidelity from those who feed on the body and blood of Christ and become one body in him. Paul agrees that idols are not real, but the demonic powers involved in worshiping any other being besides God are very real. Thus Paul teaches: "You cannot drink the cup of the Lord and the cup of demons; you cannot partake of the table of the Lord and the table of demons" (v. 21). The intimate union we share with Christ in the Eucharist demands total loyalty and the exclusive devotion of covenant.

In this teaching Paul shows us that partaking in Communion unites us with Christ, and thereby unites us to one another as his church. The early church considered both aspects important for a full understanding of the Eucharist. Because the one bread of the Eucharist is truly the body of Christ, we become the body of Christ by partaking in the body of Christ. The Eucharist is a sign of unity in Christ and deepens that unity. The church is not just a human organization, but truly the mystical body of Christ in the world. Receiving Communion, therefore, is not a solitary experience in which we shut out all others except Christ. Our "Amen" in response to the words "The Body of Christ" is our "yes" to Christ and to all who are joined to him.

Early in the fifth century, St. Augustine beautifully expressed both aspects of Communion. In teaching the newly baptized that the Eucharist is truly the body and blood of Christ, he said:

> That bread which you see on the altar, having been sanctified by the word of God, is the body of Christ. That chalice, or rather, what is in that chalice, having been sanctified by the word of God, is the blood of Christ. Through that bread and wine the Lord Christ willed to commend His body and blood, which He poured out for us unto the forgiveness of sins. If you receive worthily, you are what you have received. (St. Augustine, *Sermons*, 227)

In another sermon, Augustine expressed the reality that Communion unites us to one another as the body of Christ. He urged Christians to become what they receive:

It is your sacrament that is placed on the table of the Lord; it is your sacrament that you receive.... You hear the words, "the body of Christ," and respond "Amen." Be then a member of the body of Christ that your *Amen* may be true. (St. Augustine, *Sermons*, 272)

REFLECTING

Reflect on the truths contained in Paul's writings and how they help us understand the full significance of receiving the body and blood of Christ in Communion.

- In this passage, Paul makes a comparison between the Christian Eucharist, Israelite sacrifices, and pagan sacrifices. All of them involve a sacrificial ritual that includes partaking in a special meal of what was sacrificed. How does this comparison deepen my understanding of the sacred meal of Communion?

- Like the Israelites who were fed bread from heaven in the wilderness, we are given the living bread of Christ to be our strength for the journey. We don't stand alone before God, but we gather as Christ's church. In what ways do I experience unity in the body of Christ when I share in Communion?

- When I say "Amen" to "The body of Christ" and "The blood of Christ" at Communion, what am I affirming? How do Paul and Augustine help me to understand the fullness of my Amen?

PRAYING

Pray in response to what you have heard and understood through Paul's first letter to the Corinthians.

- Lord Jesus, when our Israelite ancestors ate the sacrifices offered on the altar, they became partners with God and with one another in covenant. As we feed on your body and blood, unite us more closely in you so that we may be your living body to one another.

Continue to pray in your heart as the Holy Spirit prompts you.

ACTING

Plan how you wish to respond to your fuller understanding of Communion.

- St. Augustine said, "Behold what you are. Become what you receive." In receiving Communion, we pray that we may be changed to be more like Christ, a change that will be fully unveiled when our bodies are resurrected and glorified like his. What does receiving Christ in the Eucharist oblige me to do in this life?

Blessing and Commissioning God's People

LISTENING

Listen to these final words of the gospels of Matthew and Luke as Jesus departs from his disciples. Consider the expectation and hope these texts offer to you.

Matthew 28:16–20

¹⁶Now the eleven disciples went to Galilee, to the mountain to which Jesus had directed them. ¹⁷When they saw him, they worshiped him; but some doubted. ¹⁸And Jesus came and said to them, "All authority in heaven and on earth has been given to me. ¹⁹Go therefore and make disciples of all nations, baptizing them in the name of the Father and of the Son and of the Holy Spirit, ²⁰and teaching them to obey everything that I have commanded you. And remember, I am with you always, to the end of the age."

Luke 24:50–53

⁵⁰Then he led them out as far as Bethany, and, lifting up his hands, he blessed them. ⁵¹While he was blessing them, he withdrew from them and was carried up into heaven. ⁵²And they worshiped him, and returned to Jerusalem with great joy; ⁵³and they were continually in the temple blessing God.

UNDERSTANDING

Try to understand these farewell texts of the gospels and how they can help us better celebrate the Concluding Rites of the Mass.

A nonbeliever once said to a Christian, "If I could believe as you believe that God is really there on the altar, I think I would fall on my knees and stay there forever." Though we must not remain on our knees because God has given us responsibilities in the world, we can maintain an orientation toward the eucharistic presence of Christ. We can continue to experience the Lord's presence in our hearts as we work, travel, and care for our families. The Eucharist is not only a personal gift but a responsibility we have to the world around us.

As the ministry of Jesus begins in each of the gospels, Jesus calls his disciples together. They listen to his teachings, share in his ministry, and witness his death and resurrection. As his ministry ends, Jesus sends his disciples outward with their mission to the world. The departure of Jesus at the end of the gospels is not a farewell but a new beginning. At the conclusion of Matthew's gospel, Jesus sends his disciples forth to evangelize, baptize, and preach, knowing that he is always with them. The gospel of Luke concludes as Jesus blesses his disciples and departs from them. But they wait with great joy for the coming of the Holy Spirit, who will impel them outward from Jerusalem to the ends of the earth.

The same two movements that characterize the beginning and the end of Jesus' ministry in the gospels form the Introductory Rites and the Concluding Rites of the Mass. As the eucharistic liturgy begins, we are gathered together to listen to God's word and to give God thanks and praise through the paschal mystery of Christ. At the end of the liturgy we are sent outward. Having encountered our eucharistic Lord and been transformed by him, we no longer want to live for ourselves but for him, and the world around us becomes our field of mission. Our worship of God in the Mass is an act of adoration, submission, and thanksgiving, but it is also a loving acceptance of our vocation as disciples. That's why every eucharistic liturgy ends on a missionary note — we are sent out, commissioned to share the treasure we have discovered with everyone we meet.

The Mass concludes with the priest's blessing and the challenge to go forth and live what we have celebrated. The community that has gathered for the Eucharist becomes the scattered community, sent forth to discover Christ in the world and amplify his presence there. While the Eucharist has concluded, our worship has not. We go in order to live the mystery we have just celebrated, through the splendor of our ordinary lives in the home and in the world.

The word "Mass" actually comes from the ancient Latin dismissal, "Ite, missa est." Literally, *missa* is indeed a sending forth, but its Christian liturgical usage implies a "mission." These final words of the Eucharist are a succinct expression of the missionary nature of the church. We are sent away from every Mass both dismissed and commissioned. These words help us to grasp the relationship between the Mass just celebrated and the mission of Christians in the world. We are sent forth on a mission to live out the challenges of the gospel in the varied ways God has called us.

In order to emphasize this missional dimension of the Eucharist, three new dismissals have been added to the traditional one in the Roman Missal. These four alternative dismissals are now translated in the following ways: "Go forth, the Mass is ended"; "Go and announce the Gospel of the Lord"; "Go in peace, glorifying the Lord by your life"; and "Go in peace." Each one of these stresses the fact, not only that the Mass is ended, but that we must now go forth, letting the mystery we have celebrated take root in our daily lives.

A renewed eucharistic spirituality enables us to see the liturgy as a school of sacrificial love. With a vision of life lived from the Eucharist and for the Eucharist, we are able to see our lives in light of God's plan for the world, in light of God's desire that all people be saved and come to the knowledge of the truth. Our mission is to testify to Jesus Christ, to make his teachings known, to struggle against all that violates God's holiness and justice in the world. With this eucharistic vision, the work of our lives takes part in God's redemptive plan in which Christ continues to reconcile all things, until that day when every knee in heaven and on earth will bend in worship.

In the Catholic vision of history, God's plan of salvation is destined to culminate in a cosmic liturgy in which all creation gives praise and glory to God, the Creator of all things. We have a foretaste of the liturgical consummation of history every time we celebrate the liturgy on earth. Each of us must make his or her own unique contribution to God's loving plan — that all creation become adoration and sacrifice in praise of him. This truth should transform the way we worship. It should move us to strive for liturgies that are reverent and beautiful, to truly live our lives as a spiritual offering to God, and to be grateful that our God would grant us the privilege of being a part of his plan to save the world.

REFLECTING

Reflect on the final words and actions of the liturgy in light of Christ's life and the mission he has given to us.

- Jesus Christ rose from the dead on "the first day of the week." For that reason, Christians hallowed Sunday as the "weekly Easter" or "the Day of the Lord." Our secular culture has so impacted our Eucharist that we no longer see Sunday as the first day of the week but as the final day of our "weekend." What if we began to see the Mass as the spiritual offering we make as we begin each week rather than something we "fit in" to our leisure activities? What impact would this have on the way I worship and the way I live my faith in the world?

- The General Instruction of the Roman Missal specifies that brief announcements, if they are necessary, should be given at the beginning of the Concluding Rites. Why are these messages about the life of the parish and community most appropriately spoken here, rather than at the beginning or in the middle of Mass?

- Liturgical renewal is the ongoing task of the church in every age. Sometimes it takes the form of structural change, but it always involves interior renewal within the hearts and minds of God's people. What changes in understanding have occurred within me during this study?

PRAYING

Respond in prayer to your listening, understanding, and reflecting.

- Lord God, you send us forth from the liturgy to announce the good news of Christ and to give you glory through our lives. Help us to live the mystery we celebrate so that we may give you thanks in all we do. Give us your peace as we await the banquet of your kingdom in the age to come.

Continue asking God for whatever you need to live your life for his glory.

ACTING

Consider how you wish to respond to your study of the Mass in Scripture.

- How have I come to realize the central place of the eucharistic liturgy in God's plan for salvation? How will my renewed eucharistic spirituality help me embrace my responsibility for the church's mission in the world?

Group Session Guide for Section VI

Begin with hospitality and welcome. Offer any announcements or instructions before entering the spirit of focused discussion. Discuss these questions or those of your own choosing:

1. Why is it essential to understand the Eucharist both as a sacrifice and a banquet? Why should these two aspects of the Mass never be separated in our understanding?

2. What is the essential purpose of the prayers and rituals of the Communion Rite?

3. What are some phrases from the Lord's Prayer that have taken on new meaning for you as you study them in the context of the Mass? (Lesson 25)

4. What does Paul mean when he says at the end of his letters, "Greet one another with a holy kiss"? (Lesson 26)

5. What have you learned about the primary meaning of the Sign of Peace? Why is it appropriately placed between the Lord's Prayer and the Fraction rite? (Lesson 26)

6. What are some of the main reasons Jesus Christ is called the Lamb of God in the church's liturgy? (Lesson 27)

7. Immediately before receiving Communion, we pray, "Lord, I am not worthy that you should enter under my roof, but only say the word and my soul shall be healed." What is the biblical context and the deeper meaning of our response? (Lesson 27)

8. How does the eucharistic discourse of Jesus in John's gospel deepen your faith in the real presence of Jesus in Communion? (Lesson 28)

9. Why are the church's beliefs about the real presence of Jesus Christ in the Eucharist so difficult to accept and so divisive for Christians? (Lesson 28)

10. How does Paul and Augustine help you understand that Communion intimately unites us both to Christ and to all others in the Christian assembly? (Lesson 29)

11. In what ways is the structure of the Mass similar to the movements of Jesus' ministry in the gospels? (Lesson 30)

12. How do the words of dismissal at the conclusion of Mass help you embrace your responsibility for the church's mission in the world? (Lesson 30)

Discuss whether or not the group would like to continue their learning with another book in the *Lectio Divina Bible Study* series.

Offer prayers of thanksgiving aloud to God for the insights and understanding you gained in the lesson this week.

Offer prayers for your own needs and the needs of others. Pray for the grace to act upon any decisions or resolutions you have made during your study.

Conclude together: *Glory be to the Father, and to the Son, and to the Holy Spirit …*